Exploring
Apologetics

Selected Readings

 Christian Schools International
Grand Rapids, Michigan

CHRISTIAN SCHOOLS INTERNATIONAL
3350 East Paris Ave., S.E.
Grand Rapids, Michigan 49512

© 1992 CHRISTIAN SCHOOLS INTERNATIONAL
Printed in the United States of America

10 9 8 7 6 5 4 3

ISBN 0-87463-882-8

The development of *Exploring Apologetics: Selected Readings* was made possible with grants from Christian Schools International Foundation and Canadian Christian Education Foundation, Inc. Cover design by Judy Zylstra.

Table of Contents

WORLDVIEWS

COMMON OBJECTIONS TO
THE CHRISTIAN FAITH

Introductory Readings

How Can I Believe in Such an Exclusive Religion?

How Can I Believe in a God Who Allows Evil and Suffering?

Do You Really Expect Me to Believe in Miracles?

Why Should I Believe That Jesus Is Anything More Than a Good Man or a Great Teacher?

Foreword

Is Christianity logical or reasonable? How can we explain why we believe in God? Is it possible to defend our beliefs when we encounter challenges to our faith from unbelievers? These are questions that many Christians have wrestled with, and this book includes some of the answers that have been suggested.

The readings in this collection are divided into three main parts. The first section discusses worldviews, perspectives that influence our understanding of reality. The second section considers some of the common objections to Christianity and offers some possible answers to the arguments. The third section contains affirmations of faith by four different authors.

Some of the readings in this book were originally written as articles; others appeared in full-length books. The readings were selected to give a broad cross section of views on these important and life-changing topics. Each reading is introduced by a short section introducing the author. After each reading is a list of questions to help you review the author's main ideas and to consider and evaluate the author's point of view.

The selection of essays was made by the editorial staff at Christian Schools International; Hazel Timmer was the general editor for the project.

It is our hope that the readings in this book will help you gain a better understanding of how to explain or defend your beliefs, and that you will be able to affirm your faith in Christ with confidence and conviction.

1
Worldviews

Worldviews: An Overview

James W. Sire

James Sire is a campus lecturer and editor for InterVarsity Press. In this selection, Sire introduces us to the concept of worldviews. A worldview is the set of beliefs which a person holds about the basic makeup of the world. In other words, what is really real and how does that relate to what we see around us in nature? Sire says there are only three basic worldviews: (1) theism, (2) naturalism, and (3) pantheism. He explains how the Christian (theistic) worldview is the only truly consistent, coherent, and rational option.

The Christian world view is only one among many in today's world. These mental models vary from culture to culture, society to society, and even from person to person. In the twentieth century, world views have in fact proliferated so much that we call our Western world pluralistic. Our culture has become almost as chaotic as the society depicted in the book of Judges. We, each of us, simply think and do whatever is right in our own eyes.

We all operate our lives out of our own mental model of the world, our own notion of what the world is really like. In other words, each of us has a world view.

What Is a World View?

What is a world view? Essentially this: *A world view is a set of presuppositions (assumptions which may be true, partially true or entirely false) which we hold (consciously or subconsciously, consistently or inconsistently) about the basic makeup of our world.*

Let us take up each part of this definition separately. A world view is set of *presuppositions*, that is, a combination of fundamental commitments to the way we think things are. In a major sense these presuppositions are pre-theoretical. We do not first get them by thinking about them. Rather, when we come to think about them, we find them already there, already undergirding any thinking we do. Of course, when we have once turned our attention to them, we can begin to think about them and consciously change them, if we wish. But at first, we just identify that we have them and then discover what they are.

Seven Basic World-View Questions

Next we note that these presuppositions are multiple; they form a *set of assumptions* that are the foundation of all our thought. The set itself can best be understood as our rock-bottom answers to seven basic questions. . . .

1. *What is prime reality—the really real?* To this different people might answer: God, or the gods, material cosmos or cosmic mind.

2. *What is the nature of external reality, that is, the world around us?* Here different people's answers point to whether They see the world as created or autonomous; as chaotic or orderly; as matter or spirit. They also show whether they emphasize a subjective, personal relationship to the world or its objectivity apart from us.

3. *What is a human being?* To this different people might answer a highly complex machine, a sleeping god, a person made in the image of God, a "naked ape."

4. *What happens to a person at death?* Here different people might reply: personal extinction, or transformation to a higher state, or departure to a shadowy existence on "the other side."

5. *Why is it possible to know anything at all?* Sample answers include the idea that human beings are made in the image of an all-knowing God or that consciousness and rationality developed under the contingencies of survival in a long process of evolution.

6. *How do we know what is right and wrong?* Again, perhaps we are made in the image of a God whose character is good; or right and wrong are determined by human choice alone;

or the notions simply developed under an impetus toward cultural or physical survival.

7. *What is the meaning of human history?* To this different people might answer: to realize the purposes of God or the gods, to make a paradise on earth, to prepare a people for a life in community with a loving and holy God, and so forth.

Randomness or evolving to a higher sphere.

More or Less Conscious, True, Consistent

Our own personal answers to these questions are our world view. But what a set of questions! They strike us with their depth, with the mystery that lies at the base of our answers to them, whatever those answers are. They are the toughest questions of life. So tough that, when we reflect on them, we may well give up trying to make sense of or be confident of our answers. That is, we are only more or less *conscious* of our world view.

Often in the process of growing up, we raise these questions with our parents or teachers or friends, and they look away embarrassed. They, no more than you, know how to answer them. Thus as children we often cease asking these questions of others and even of ourselves. Our budding critical mind shuts down. Cultural forces mold our actions and beliefs and, unless some crisis of life comes along—our best friend dies young, our own children go on drugs, we discover we have cancer—we never bother to ask the questions again.

By the time we are fully grown, even through college and into the workaday world, we may not be conscious of our answers to some of them at all. As Whitehead says, some "assumptions appear so obvious that people do not know what they are assuming because no other way of putting things has ever occurred to them."

I suspect, for example, that most people today have at least once in their lifetime thought about whether God exists and, if not, then wondered how the universe came into being or continues to hang together. And many have wondered how they could find the answers to their questions about this. They have thought about gathering data and maybe making hypotheses about that data and then confirming their hypotheses with further thought and experiment. In other words, they may have a conscious grasp of some elements of the so-called scientific method and have thought about applying it to the question of God's existence. But I suspect that few have consciously asked how it is possible to know anything at all. We just know, don't we?

Moreover, each presupposition we make, each answer we give to these questions, is more or less *true*. Any given assumption we make about what is finally there—God or the universe or cosmic mind—is either true, partially true (needing considerable refinement) or entirely false. The notion, for example, that the universe is upheld by the Downers Grove frog god is certainly false. But does an infinite-personal God, say Yahweh or Allah, uphold the universe? That is not so easy to determine. Still, either he does or he doesn't, and the presupposition that he does is either true or false (or in need of further clarification so that we can be sure what is being asserted).

Finally, our presuppositions are either more or less *consistent* with each other. Some people, for example, do not believe in the supernatural or in the existence of a spiritual realm, yet they take comfort in the idea of reincarnation. But reincarnation implies precisely what the existence of either the supernatural or the spiritual realm affirms—a substratum of existence that is not material. They can't have it both ways. Some Christians have tried to blend reincarnation with their otherwise orthodox notions of God and human nature, and that cannot be done consistently either.

The Christian World View

The Christian world view answers each of the seven questions with a fair degree of confidence. It claims the answers are true and consistent with each other. In light of all the confusion regarding these questions today, how is this possible? The world view itself explains why. God wants us to know these answers, and he has told us what the answers are.

The Christian world view's answer to the first question

forms the basis for the answers to all the other questions, for what the Christian world view takes to be the really real is an infinite-personal God who intentionally made the universe and us in it. He wanted us around to freely know him, and so he built into us the capacity for knowledge.

But this is to get way ahead of ourselves. We need to back up before going on. The question of just what fundamental reality is is prior to how we know what fundamental reality is. So let us begin at the beginning.

The Beginning That Has No Beginning

What is the beginning that has no beginning? Sounds like a riddle Rumpelstiltskin might ask—a conundrum, needing an answer like a circle or a sphere. Instead, it is the most important question our world view answers. The answer determines the shape of every answer to every other world-view question. Essentially what this question demands of us is a commitment to reality. After all that is finite and contingent has been transcended, what is the world like at its rootiest root? It is, in other words, a formulation of the first of two questions we will deal with in this chapter. Let's get them out on the table.

Question 1: What is prime reality—the really real?
Question 2: What is the nature of external reality, that is, the world around us? What kind of place do we live in, anyway?

An Elephant Story

There is a story that places these first two world-view questions in perspective.

One day a little boy came to his father and asked, "You know, Dad, our teacher just showed us that the world is really round and that it is just out there alone. Gee, Dad, what holds it up?"

His father thinking his son would be satisfied with a

child's answer, said, "Well, son, a camel holds the world up." His son, always trusting his father, looked puzzled but walked away satisfied—for a while.

The next day after he thought this over, he came back to his Dad and asked the obvious question. "Dad, you know, you said yesterday the world rests on a camel. But what holds the camel up?"

His father, a bit perplexed, quickly thought, "You know, this kid's got a good question. I don't know the answer to it, but I'd better make up one—and fast." Like most fathers he knew instinctively that a quick answer turneth away further questions. So he said with confidence, "Son, a kangaroo holds the camel up."

So his son went away but returned a short time later and said, "Hey, Dad. I've still got a problem. What holds up the kangaroo?"

His father was now desperate, so he thought quickly and figured he would make one last try. So he searched his mind for the largest animal he could think of, and he put a capital on it and said loudly (if you shout, people believe you): "An Elephant holds the world up."

"Come on, Dad," his son said, having now caught on that his father was not getting to the bottom of things, "what holds up the Elephant?"

So his father came back in an exasperated stroke of pure genius, "Son, it's Elephant all the way down."

A Sure-fire Test for Presuppositions

This story illustrates two very important ideas. First, it illustrates what a presupposition is. You know you have reached a presupposition when the only thing left to do is shout. A child asks, "Why, Mamma?" and eventually, after all the explanation she can give proves unsuccessful, she is forced to declare in a question-stopping voice: "Because! Just because!" One cannot endlessly pile animal after animal, reason after reason, on top of each other. One reaches a point at which there seems no way to go further. One cannot prove to oneself that that point is the final resting place. One just has to say, "That's it. I can go no further with my explanations. This will have to suffice until I think of something better."

Sagan or Kepler

Second. the Elephant story illustrates the kind of answer that applies to the first world-view question: *What is prime reality—the really real.* The question "What holds up the world?" is simply another way of asking, What is the basis for the way things are? What is the final reality that explains how things hold together?

Let us see what would have happened if the father in the Elephant story had taken an adult, say, scientific approach. Let's say that he had said to his son's first question, "The law of gravity holds the world in place."

"Gosh, Dad, what's that?"

"Well, it's rather complicated to explain, and it took us as a human race a long time to figure it out. But about three hundred years ago Isaac Newton finally did. The basic idea is this: $F = G(m_1 m_2)/R^2$. This obtains where F = the force of gravity; G = the gravitational constant; m_1 = the mass of body l; m_2 = the mass of body 2; and R = the distance between m_1 and m_2."

"Wow, Dad. That's impressive. But why is this so?"

His father could then say, "The law of gravity works because it is the expression of the uniformity of natural causes operating in the universe. You see, the universe is an orderly place. Things always work the same way under the same conditions. The law of gravity simply expresses the principle of uniformity as regards the relationship between physical bodies in the universe."

Would not his son again ask, "Why, Dad?"

His father then would have to make a choice. He could end the discussion in one of two ways. He could say, "Well, that's just the way it is. That is the foundation principle of the universe: it's uniform all the way down." That is, he could commit himself to the final reality being the orderly structure of the material universe. That is in fact what I think astrophysicist and scientific popularizer Carl Sagan would tell his son, for Sagan opens his book and his TV series *Cosmos* with just such a statement: "The Cosmos is all there is or ever was or ever will be."

But there is a second possibility. He could go one step further, saying, "Well, son that's the way God made the world. Isn't it wonderful! God is a rational God. The Bible even calls him Logos, logic itself. So, of course, the world is orderly!" This is what scientist Johannes Kepler would have told his son, for he once wrote in praise of God the Creator, "O God, I am thinking thy thoughts after thee."

Given the assumption that the earth and other astral bodies are really "out there" as objective, material entities (a view which is possible to challenge, as we shall see in a moment), I don't see what other alternatives would be available. Either the world is orderly on its own, or it has been brought into being by a God who wanted it to be orderly. Either answer on the surface of it is possible. Neither answer can be proven. Both are presuppositions, pretheoretical commitments. As such they may both be tested—that is, one could see what follows from each, and one of them might emerge as more likely to be the case than the other, but it is in principle impossible to get beneath either. To do so would be to be God, to be within oneself cognizant of eternal matters.

The Great Divide: Theism, Naturalism or Pantheism

Though the variations within them are many indeed, in my estimation there are only three basic world views. When we answer the first world-view question, we have no choice but to commit ourselves to one of these views. In the Elephant story and its commentary we have seen the beginnings of two of them. The third we will introduce presently.

Theists like Kepler say that prime reality is an infinite-personal God. He alone exists forever. All that is not this God is the creation of this God.

Naturalists like Sagan say that prime reality is the cosmos itself.

"Cosmos is God"

Pantheists, at least one major segment of them, say prime reality is Brahman, the divine oneness that unifies everything. That is, God and the Cosmos are really one and the same.

The pantheist's answer may seem odd because the cosmos does not look like God to us. But that is so, the pantheist would say, because under ordinary circumstances (that is, when we trust our senses and our ability to reason), we are not actually in touch with reality. Our senses, including those that perceive the world as "out there" in space, separated from other astral bodies, are misleading us. The earth does not need to be held up by anything. The whole so-called physical universe is an illusion.

In terms of the Elephant story, a father who is this sort of pantheist might answer his son's question about what holds the world in space this way.

"Son, the earth, you know, is not really there at all. It is not so much hanging in space in and of itself as it simply appears to you and your teacher to be so."

"What do you mean, Dad? How is that an answer."

"There are no answers, Son. There should be no questions."

"Why, Dad?"

"That's a question, Son. You must learn not to ask questions."

"How, Dad?"

"There you go again! Come, let us sit together quietly. Let us breathe deeply, quietly. Let us look at this beautiful design, Son."

The end of such an approach is to put questions of all kinds on hold. To those of us raised in the Western world, the whole process seems wrong-headed. But it is taken very seriously by much of the world's population, and it has a sophisticated literature and a vast panorama of religious expressions. Hinduism and Buddhism in the many forms are fueled by this fundamental commitment to the notion that everything either is God, an emanation of God or total illusion. We look at other forms of pantheism below in this chapter.

On the basis of their answer to the first world-view question, then, we have three possible basic world views. These can be diagrammed as in figure 1.

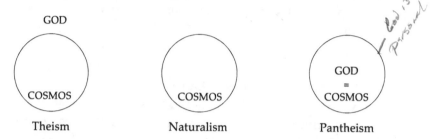

Figure 1. God and cosmos in theism, naturalism and pantheism.

God as the Really Real

Christianity is obviously a form of theism, though it is not the only example of theism. Two other major religions are theistic—Judaism and Islam. Within both these religions God is seen as prime reality. All else stems from him.

The differences between these three religions have to do with the character and nature of this God who is believed to exist. Christianity and Islam both accept much of the Hebrew Scripture's notion of God—his infinity, his absolute power, his sovereignty over his own creation, including humanity. But Islam holds that Muhammad was God's special prophet who wrote the Koran by direct dictation from God and so the teachings of the Koran take precedence over the Hebrew Scriptures. Christianity, on the other hand, sees God as Trinity—Father, Son and Holy Spirit—and it emphasizes the incarnation of God the Son as Jesus Christ, who expressed God's love by dying for the sins of the people he created. Christians see both the teachings of Jesus and his apostles and the Hebrew Scriptures as authoritative.

In any case, it is not the differences between these forms of theism that will occupy us here. The important matter is the development of a Christian mind. So we will focus on the nature of God as Christians view him.

The God of the Old and New Testaments is *infinite* and *per-*

sonal (Triune), transcendent and immanent, sovereign, omniscient and good. One classic Protestant definition of God is found in the Westminster Confession:

> There is but one living and true God, who is infinite in being and perfection, a most pure spirit, invisible, without body, parts or passions, immutable, immense, eternal, incomprehensible, almighty; most wise, most holy, most free, most absolute, working all things according to the counsel of his own immutable and most righteous will, for his own glory; most loving, gracious, merciful, long-suffering, abundant in goodness and truth, forgiving iniquity, transgression and sin; the rewarder of them that diligently seek him; and withal most just and terrible in his judgments; hating all sin, and who will by no means clear the guilty.

We saw in the Elephant story a little of what it means for God to be *infinite.* He is the final reality, the only self-existent being. As Jehovah God spoke to Moses out of the burning bush, "I AM WHO I AM" (Ex 3:14). He *is* in a way that none else is. As Moses proclaimed, "Hear, O Israel: The LORD our God, the LORD is one" (Deut 6:4). So God is the one prime existent, the one prime reality and, as we shall develop later, the one source of all other reality.

God is *personal.* This means God is not mere force or energy or existent "substance." Rather, he has the two basic characteristics of personality: (1) self-reflection and (2) self-determination. He knows himself to be, and he is an agent of action. He is not compelled by anything external to himself but can freely determine what he wishes and act as he chooses.

The personhood of God is expressed in the *Trinity,* three "persons," Father, Son and Holy Spirit, yet one as God. As theologian Geoffrey W. Bromiley says, "Within the one essence of the Godhead we have to distinguish three 'persons' who are neither three gods on the one side, not three parts or modes of God on the other, but coequally and coeternally God." The Trinity confirms the communal, "personal" nature of ultimate being. God is not only there—an actually existent being—he is personal, and we can relate to him in a personal way.

God is also *transcendent*. This means God is beyond us and our world. He is *otherly*. He is not a part of the cosmos, nor are we a part of him. The ancient Hebrew psalmist wrote,

> I lift up my eyes to the hills—
>   where does my help come from?

And he quickly answers,

> My help comes from the Lord,
>   the Maker of heaven and earth. (Ps 121:1-2)

There has been a long and deep strain of pantheism in human history even in the West. Think, for example, of William Wordsworth, in England, and Ralph Waldo Emerson, Henry David Thoreau and Walt Whitman, in America, and more recently the literature of the beat generation—Jack Kerouac and Gary Snyder. Nature for these authors takes on a cast of the divine. It would be from the spirit of the hills themselves that these authors would seek help. But the God of the Bible is transcendent. God is not the hills; he is beyond them. He is otherly, as some theologians put it.

Yet it is still true that God is constantly present to all his creation. God is indeed not only transcendent but *immanent* as well. Look at a hill: God is present. Look at a person: God is present. Is this, then, a contradiction? Is theism nonsense at this point? I think not.

Is God *here* in the same way a hill is here? No, not quite. God is immanent, here, everywhere, in a sense completely in line with his transcendence. For God is not *matter*, but Spirit. A text from the book of Hebrews states it this way: Jesus Christ is said to be "upholding the universe by his word of power" (Heb 1:3 RSV). That is, God is beyond all, yet in all and sustaining all.

God is also *sovereign*. This is really a further ramification of God's infiniteness, but it expresses more fully his concern to rule, to pay attention, as it were, to all the actions of his universe. It expresses the fact that nothing is beyond God's ultimate interest, control and authority.

God is likewise both *omniscient* and *good*.

And that brings us to the second world-view question: What is the nature of external reality?

We will begin to answer the second question by making a comparison again between the three world views. This time we will look at other forms of pantheism than the one we have just seen above. But let's take the simplest one first.

The Cosmos on Its Own

Naturalists hold that the cosmos itself is eternal. That means that for the naturalist the answer to the first two world-view questions is the same.

True, the cosmos has not always been in its present form, and its form is constantly changing, at least from our point of view. But the natural order of things (the matter/energy complex)—that is all there is. The cosmos is closed off from any influence from the outside; in fact, there is no outside. There is a uniformity of natural causes in a totally closed system. In such a system, of course, there can be no miracle. Anything that looks a miracle is merely the result of natural causes we have not yet understood.

For naturalists, therefore, all explanations of how things are have to be made in terms of the natural order. If something moves, it moves because of its place in the natural scheme. If someone has an idea, it is because of the inherent character of the natural world. If someone believes there is something outside the cosmos, then that belief must be explained in terms of the natural world. God is never seen to be the cause of the idea of God. Rather the idea of a God outside the cosmos is caused by something within the cosmos itself. Naturalists, therefore, have sociologies of religion and psychologies of religion (the subject of both of which include belief in God) but never theologies (for theologies have God for their subject and God doesn't exist).

This fact, by the way, explains the frequent frustration of many Christians who study social science in the university. It seems to them as if their religious views are never taken as

serious contenders for truth. This is so not because their teachers have it in for them, so to speak, but because these teachers
have ruled out from the start any possibility that any religious
idea could be true. We have here what Stephen Eyre calls the
socialization of unbelief. When Christian students understand
this, they can get on with the task of learning from their courses despite the prejudice against their views. The fact is that
their teachers are often ignorant of the contributions of
thoughtful Christians to the social sciences. And many as well
are ignorant of what genuine biblical Christianity is.

The Cosmos as Divine

Pantheists, at least a very large portion of them, hold that
the external world is really illusory. The cosmos is a projection
of God, somehow equal to God, in as much as it exists, but
totally illusory as objective in and of itself.

The key phrase in this form of pantheism is *Atman is Brahman,* a phrase coming from The Upanishads, one of the Hindu
scriptures. That is, Atman (the soul of any one person or thing)
is Brahman (God, the Soul of everything). In the non-dualist
form of pantheism, all things in as much as they are differenti-
ated from each other are illusory. Brahman (prime reality) is
one and one alone. Sometimes the external world is said to be
the dream of God or an emanation from God or an extension
of God. It is not, however, God's creation; it is, in as much as it
is at all, a part of God. Of course, because Brahman is the uni-
tary one, it is also appropriate to say the external universe is
not Brahman but rather illusion.

Do not be discouraged if you have found the above two
paragraphs difficult to comprehend. The nondualist form of
pantheism (one of its major expressions) is not capable of
being understood by normal intellectual processes. One has to
pass, so these pantheists say, beyond the mind and grasp the
matter intuitively. Meditation replaces thought as a way of getting to the bottom of things.

There are other ways of formulating the pantheist answer
to what is the really real. The Buddhists, for instance, take a

radically different notion of what this oneness at the root of reality is. For them it is the Void—the nothingness from which all illusory forms come. Each person, each self, is not Atman (soul); each self is really not-self, a kind of undifferentiated nothingness. From such a conception stems a very different form of religion (if Buddhism can be called a religion, since it really does not believe in any kind of God at all).

One can also hold dualist forms of pantheism. Here God and the cosmos are held to be the same, but genuine existence is granted to a multiplicity of forms. Animism—the idea that nature has a divine substratum, that spirits live in trees, rivers and all natural forms—is a subspecies of pantheism that does not so much emphasize the unity of reality as its diversity. Some "nature lovers" too modern to believe that spirits live in trees nonetheless see nature itself as divine. Animals (baby seals and whales, for example) have as much right to life as we.

One of the most interesting forms pantheism has taken recently is the Gaia hypothesis. Gaia is the name of the ancient Greek Earth goddess. Some scientists are proposing that the Earth itself is somehow alive, a single giant organism, or maybe even a single cell, of which the various life forms are a part. Biologist and medical doctor Lewis Thomas muses:

> I have been trying to think of the earth as a kind of organism, but it is no go. I cannot think of it this way. It is too big, too complex, with too many working parts lacking visible connections. The other night, driving through a hilly, wooded part of southern New England, I wondered about this. If not like an organism, what is it like, what is it *most* like? Then, satisfactorily for that moment, it came to me: it is *most* like a single cell."

This single cell, in Thomas's musings, begins to take on the characteristics of at least a lesser God. He talks of DNA being an *invention* of nature *designed* for a specific task, of human beings as made for a purpose—to have language that is ambiguous so that we can invent and imagine and create. And he even speculates that at death the human consciousness is "somehow separated off at the filaments of its attachment, and then drawn like an easy breath back into the membrane of its origin, a fresh memory for the biospherical nervous system." Then tellingly he adds, "but I have no data on the matter."

Lewis comes close to talking about a cosmic mind, a thoughtfulness in the universe, a central controlling intelligence which, while it may not be fully personal or endowed with loving intentions, nonetheless "holds up the world" and suggests a modicum of purpose to reality. What ever form it takes, pantheism, without recognizing the existence of a transcendent God, endows the cosmos with the aura of divinity.

The Cosmos as Created

Theists hold that the external world is a deliberate, designed orderly creation of God over which his sovereignty continues to extend.

The opening text of the Bible says it most succinctly: "In the beginning God created the heavens and the earth" (Gen 1:1). The verses that follow give an account of the orderly progression of God's creative activity. And Isaiah echoes this in many ways, not the least in this passage:

I am the LORD,
who has made all things,
who alone stretched out the heavens,
who spread out the earth by myself. (Is 44:24)

It is a view made for poetry, and Scripture abounds in rhapsodic song:

O LORD my God, you are very great;
    you are clothed with splendor and majesty.
He wraps himself in light as with a garment;
    he stretches out the heavens like a tent
        and lays the beams of his upper chambers on their
            waters.
He makes the clouds his chariot
    and rides on the wings of the wind.

He makes winds his messengers,
> flames of fire his servants.
He set the earth on its foundations;
> it can never be moved. (Ps 104:1-5)

Notice how the last line, without stopping to contemplate the role of gravity (Newtonian or Einsteinian), simply answers our young boy's question. Who holds the world in place? God himself. He made it. He takes care of it.

The heavens declare the glory of God;
> the skies proclaim the work of his hands. (Ps 19:1)

The notion of God as Creator, however, is not just a matter for poetic ecstasy. There is no notion more important to the Christian mind than the notion of God as Creator. Let us look at *two* reasons this is so.

First, the notion of God as Creator puts us in our place. God is God; we are not. Everything we are and have belongs to him. We own nothing that is not his—our bodies, our souls, our minds, our emotions, our thoughts. And that is true for everyone whether they know it or not.

We cannot escape his presence. If he should forget about us, we would cease to exist. This is both terrifying and comforting.

Where can I go from your Spirit?
> Where can I flee from your presence? . . .
If I say, "Surely the darkness will hide me
> and the light become night around me,"
even the darkness will not be dark to you;
> the night will shine like the day,
> for darkness is as light to you. (Ps 139: 7,11-12)

It is terrifying to think that there is nothing God does not know about us, for what we ourselves know about us is bad enough. Our sins are an open book for him to read and weep—and worse! Even our goodness is like filthy rags (Is 64:6). But his constant presence is also comforting. It is comforting to know that God in his mercy is so gracious to us that he puts our sins as far away from him as is the east from the west (Ps 103:12). The contemplation of his presence indeed brings us to the *fear of the Lord,* which is, as we saw, the beginning of knowledge.

Second, the notion of God as Creator affects the way we think about everything. If God is really the creator of everything other than himself, then our understanding of anything will be incomplete and maybe quite inaccurate unless we take into account his presence as Creator. Upon hearing him present one of his scientific theories, Napoleon once asked P. S. Laplace (1749-1827) where God was in all of his explanation. Laplace replied, "I have no need of God in my hypotheses." Laplace may have been right, so long as he limited himself to purely physical bodies and the structure of their relationship to each other. But the bodies wouldn't be there without God, nor would Laplace or Napoleon. There would be no thought to think, no hypothesis making, no question asking, nothing at all.

Much modern thought, however, assumes that Laplace is right in the ultimate and absolute sense. Naturalism exalts Laplace's answer to a metaphysical principle. As much as we as Christians can respect much of the work of modern science, we cannot marginalize God or push him to the edge of our minds when we do science. He must be the hidden premise of all our work as scholars. He is the reason the world is orderly and therefore capable of being understood.

Third, the notion of God as creator affects the way we understand what the universe is like. God is totally free to make any kind of universe he chooses to make. It is an orderly universe because he is a rational God. But it does not have to have any specific pattern. That is, the order in his creation may not be presumed.

In medieval thought the circle was considered the perfect geometrical form. God made the heavens; the heavens, unlike the earth, are not fallen but perfect; perfect motion is motion in a circle; therefore, the orbits of the planets must be circular. Johannes Kepler went even further. He argued that since God is orderly (actually, a mathematician), then the planets must not only inscribe circular orbits, but also orbits which have a tidy but subtle relationship to the perfect solids. His particular views are too complex to be described here. The point is that the facts Kepler had available came close to justifying his theory but not close enough to constitute a proof. Finally Kepler gave up his theory in the face of the facts. When Kepler considered sufficient data, he discovered that the planets moved in elliptic, not circular orbits.

So the idea of the universe as created means that (1) it actually exists apart from any human observer and is not just an illusion; (2) it is orderly; and (3) it is contingent (its specific form is not *necessary*). As Charles Hummel says, "The dependence of such beliefs, both historically and philosophically, on the biblical doctrine of creation leads directly to the role of Christianity in the scientific revolution."

So then, what is the nature of external reality? External reality is creation. And since this creation is the result of the design of a rational God, it is orderly—*a uniformity of natural causes in an open system*. That is, in addition to being orderly, it is always open to its creator for reordering and to any personal beings to whom its creator gives power. Miracles are possible in a theistic universe because God can always do whatever he chooses. These miracles are not of course, illogical or irrational, because the creator is not illogical or irrational. They may occur seldom or often. They may be understood by people or not understood, but when the latter is the case it will not be due to the illogic of the miracle but to the inability of the human mind always to understand its maker.

The World-View Matrix

Our discussion of these first two questions illustrates an important feature of world views. The answer they give to one question affects the answers they give to all the other questions one can ask. Naturalism's answer to question 2 is in fact the same as it is to question 1. And given theism's answer to question 1, the cosmos has to have been created. For if both God and the cosmos exist now, and if the cosmos did not always exist then the only way it could have come into being is if God created it.

As Christians we want to learn, as Kepler said, to think

God's thoughts after him. God is rational; therefore, we should be rational. Our world view, then, should be both consistent and coherent. That is, not only should it not contain any contradictions, but it should be composed of presuppositions which fit well together, presuppositions which, because they are as correct as we can get them, give us a coherent picture of the way things really are.

This is a tall order—too tall to be accomplished in this lifetime. Yet we can try.

DISCUSS pg 25←

Questions

1. The author says that there are only three basic worldviews. What are they and how do they explain the existence of prime reality?
2. Describe your worldview.
3. How does the author define a presupposition?
4. Why is it important for one's worldview to be both consistent and coherent?

1.) Theism — God is at the center of all reality. He is the creator.

Naturalism — The cosmos has always been & will always be.

Pantheism — The cosmos is in fact God. God is in & runs through all things.

Pg 9
2.) My world view is Christian. God is infinite, personal, transcendent, immanent, sovereign, omniscient, and good.

Pg 9
3.) Presuppositions — Combination of fundamental commitments to the way we think things are.

Pg 28
4.) Consistency between assumptions shows coherency. This is Rational in other words our world view presuppositions fit together.

A Victim of Spiritual Poverty

Robert Coles

Robert Coles is a Pulitzer Prize-winning author and professor of psychiatry who has devoted his entire career to exploring and illuminating the inner world of children under stress. In this selection, taken from Coles' book Harvard Diary, *he describes the values and ideals of a young friend who exemplifies a certain North American worldview. As a young boy, his friend was intent on achieving material success in life. Later, in his 20s, his values had not changed. But Coles observes that despite his friend's material prosperity, he remains a victim of spiritual poverty.*

I hope I never forget him, a 12-year-old boy in New Orleans whom I got to know in the 1960s, as that city struggled with the turmoil of school desegregation. But that child was white, went to a fancy private school, and was the much-loved son of extremely rich parents. No racial crisis bore down on him, as it did on the much more vulnerable white people of that interesting old port city, not to mention the blacks who lived there in such substantial numbers. The boy already had a sense of himself—"an air of importance about him," as one of his teachers put it. When I came to visit his parents, and hear what they thought—the father was an exceedingly influential lawyer who had taken a strong interest in the progress of school desegregation—the boy would inevitably appear, approach me, and tell me (whether I asked or not) what he had on his mind. Often his comments took the form of admonitions, caveats: didn't I know that "the colored" are not "reliable," or "don't always speak so you can understand them"? When I disagreed with him, or even gently challenged him, he got huffy: I'd find out, eventually, the truths he already knew.

I kept in touch with him over the years (the 1960s and 1970s) and I did find out certain truths—what it was that characterized much of his life. They were truths he was quite willing to share with me—as in this self-regarding series of observations, made when he had turned 16: "I hate these long spring vacations. We've been everywhere! We just keep going back to places! My mother likes to see those ruins in Mexico. My father likes to go out West and ski. They fight over where to go. I just like a swimming pool in a hotel, near the ocean, with lots of different restaurants and a good tennis pro. If I have my way, I'll be the best tennis player in the world. I'll play all the tournaments! I have a pro here, but he's not good enough. I think I'll outgrow him soon. I don't like tennis camps: too many people! I like a good game with a pro who knows how to teach, but isn't too pushy.

"I don't know what I'd like to do when I'm older. I wouldn't mind 'real estate development.' I'm not sure what it is, but I hear my father's friends say you can make two or three extra fortunes in it, if you're savvy. If you're not [savvy] you have no business in it [real estate development]. I don't just want to sit on my inheritance; I know that. You've got to keep your assets growing, or you'll slip back. There's always some dude coming down the pike, ready to shove you aside and take the lead! I'd like to be up there, out in front—that's my ambition!"

In his 20s he was no less determined to "keep up there," as he'd often put it. I had known him long enough to be able to joke with him, even push him hard about his ideals and values. He is a good-natured person, and quite generous to his friends. He is also practical, earthy, and in certain respects quite unpretentious—a contrast, I often realize, with some of us politically liberal academics, whose assertively declared compassion for others is all too evenly matched by our showy self-importance, and our gossipy delight in dismissing anyone who happens to have the slightest reservations about one or another of our chosen "causes." Not least, he has continued to be ambitious: "I'd like to get a new business going—something different from all others! I'd like to see my business grow and grow, and then I'll be way up there, and my friends will pick up a copy of *Fortune* or *Business Week* or *The Wall Street Journal* and they'll see me. You're only here once, and you have to prove yourself. If you don't, then it's your loss. If you don't, you have no right to be belly aching about someone who's gone and done something and got some place. Why are people so mad, because a guy goes and makes himself a success out of life?

"You keep asking me what I want out of life, and I keep telling you—but you don't believe me! Things don't have to be as complicated as can be; they can be simple. You get an idea; you play with it, until it really makes sense; you figure out how you can go from point A to point B; you plan and plan about what you'll do then, when you're at point B and then, one day, you take the plunge, you go for broke. If you fail, you fail: you take the blame on your shoulders and you don't weep and moan and start bemoaning everyone else. If you don't fail- if you succeed—then you take the credit, and you don't start apologizing to the world, because you've come out on top! No, sir! This country became what it is because there were people who had the courage and the toughness to take risks, and to keep pushing—to have dreams, and to work hard to make the dreams come true. If we keep apologizing because of our suc- cess—if we start losing our spirit, and feeling we're bad, because we want to be rich and have some influence in the world, then we'll become a different country. We'll all have the welfare mentality before long!"

I won't easily forget probing with him that phrase "the welfare mentality." He was tolerant of me and my worries— ready to explain himself. But he was not at all inclined to yield territory—including any of the higher ground of moral convic- tion: "When people think the country—the federal govern- ment, or the city—owes them a living, they've lost all their self-respect. They've become parasites. You may think we can afford to have a lot of people like that in the country, but the more we have, the bigger the burden, and soon you have a few working hard and millions sitting and doing nothing for themselves. That would be the end of America—a disaster for the world. It would be a terrible thing for the Christian religion, too. The Communists would swallow up Christianity. My idea of what Christianity should be [is] . . . each person standing there, alone, before God, and showing Him that you have the courage to live your life to the fullest, to do the best you can with the gift he's given you: the time to spend here."

I suppose many would want to become indignant, outraged by such statements, and for understandable reasons. Perhaps because I've known this person almost his entire life (and a big hunk of my own) I feel otherwise—saddened, even a little hurt: so much intelligence and energy which never seem to be offered to others, but rather, get channeled into the various real estate deals he's learned to make. He himself describes those deals as "speculating"—for him no pejorative word, any more than the mergers and takeovers we've been observing in recent years are, for him, suspect or worse. I suppose my anger toward him takes the form of pity. I lament the direction he has taken—hear myself calling him vulnerable, needy, virtually indigent: a victim of spiritual poverty who makes me realize how morally exalted, how spiritually affluent some materially impoverished people I've met have managed to become. "We have to pray for the lost souls we see among us," Dorothy Day used to say—and then she'd always add, "and hope that we won't become one of them." One prays; one hopes.

December 1986

Questions

1. Why does the young man want to be successful in life? Is that a good reason? How does he plan to achieve success?
2. The young man says, "This country became what it is because there were people who had the courage and the

toughness to take risks, and to keep pushing—to have dreams, and to work hard to make the dreams come true." Can a person argue with that statement? Taken in its context, what does it tell you about the speaker?

3. Do you feel sorry for the young man, or would you not mind trading places with him? Why?

Origins

Desmond Morris

Desmond Morris is a writer and former zoologist whose book
The Naked Ape *attempts to explain the presence and
behavior of "the human animal." In the book he focuses on
activities shared with other species, such as feeding, groom-
ing, sleeping, fighting, mating, and care of the young. This
selection deals with* Homo sapiens' *origin and religious
practices.*

There is a label on a cage at a certain zoo that states simply,
"This animal is new to science." Inside the cage there sits a
small squirrel. It has black feet and it comes from Africa. No
blackfooted squirrel has ever been found in that continent
before. Nothing is known about it. It has no name.

For the zoologist it presents an immediate challenge. What
is it about its way of life that has made it unique? How does it
differ from the three hundred and sixty-six other living species
of squirrels already known and described? Somehow, at some
point in the evolution of the squirrel family, the ancestors of
this animal must have split off from the rest and established
themselves as an independent breeding population. What was
it in the environment that made possible their isolation as a
new form of life? The new trend must have started out in a
small way, with a group of squirrels in one area becoming
slightly changed and better adapted to the particular conditions there. But at this stage they would still be able to inter-
breed with their relatives nearby. The new form would be at a
slight advantage in its special region, but it would be no more
than a race of the basic species and could be swamped out, re-
absorbed into the mainstream at any point. If, as time passed,
the new squirrels became more and more perfectly tuned-in to

their particular environment, the moment would eventually arrive when it would be advantageous for them to become isolated from possible contamination by their neighbours. At this stage their social and sexual behaviour would undergo special modifications, making inter-breeding with other kinds of squirrels unlikely and eventually impossible. At first, their anatomy may have changed and become better at coping with the special food of the district, but later their mating calls and displays would also differ, ensuring that they attract only mates of the new type. At last, a new species would have evolved, separate and discrete, a unique form of life, a three hundred and sixty-seventh kind of squirrel.

When we look at our unidentified squirrel in its zoo cage, we can only guess about these things. All we can be certain about is that the markings of its fur—its black feet—indicate that it is a new form. But these are only the symptoms, the rash that gives a doctor a clue about his patient's disease. To really understand this new species, we must use these clues only as a starting point, telling us there is something worth pursuing. We might try to guess at the animal's history, but that would be presumptuous and dangerous. Instead we will start humbly by giving it a simple and obvious label: we will call it the African black-footed squirrel. Now we must observe and record every aspect of its behaviour and structure and see how it differs from, or is similar to, other squirrels. Then, little by little, we can piece together its story.

The great advantage we have when studying such animals is that we ourselves are not black-footed squirrels—a fact which forces us into an attitude of humility that is becoming to proper scientific investigation. How different things are, how depressingly different, when we attempt to study the human animal. Even for the zoologist, who is used to calling an animal an animal, it is difficult to avoid the arrogance of subjective involvement. We can try to overcome this to some extent by deliberately and rather coyly approaching the human being as if he were another species, a strange form of life on the dissecting table, awaiting analysis. How can we begin?

As with the new squirrel, we can start by comparing him with other species that appear to be most closely related. From his teeth, his hands, his eyes and various other anatomical features, he is obviously a primate of some sort, but of a very odd kind. Just how odd becomes clear when we lay out in a long row the skins of the one hundred and ninety-two living species of monkeys and apes, and then try to insert a human pelt at a suitable point somewhere in this long series. Wherever we put it, it looks out of place. Eventually we are driven to position it right at one end of the row of skins, next to the hides of the tailless great apes such as the chimpanzee and the gorilla. Even here it is obtrusively different. The legs are too long, the arms are too short and the feet are rather strange. Clearly this species of primate has developed a special kind of locomotion which has modified its basic form. But there is another characteristic that cries out for attention: the skin is virtually naked. Except for conspicuous tufts of hair on the head, in the armpits and around the genitals, the skin surface is completely exposed. When compared with the other primate species, the contrast is dramatic. True, some species of monkeys and apes have small naked patches of skin on their rumps, their faces, or their chests, but nowhere amongst the other one hundred and ninety-two species is there anything even approaching the human condition. At this point and without further investigation, it is justifiable to name this new species the "naked ape." It is a simple, descriptive name based on a simple observation, and it makes no special assumptions. Perhaps it will help us to keep a sense of proportion and maintain our objectivity.

Staring at this strange specimen and puzzling over the significance of its unique features, the zoologist now has to start making comparisons. Where else is nudity at a premium? The other primates are no help, so it means looking farther afield. A rapid survey of the whole range of the living mammals soon proves that they are remarkably attached to their protective, furry covering, and that very few of the 4,237 species in existence have seen fit to abandon it. Unlike their reptilian ancestors, mammals have acquired the great physiological advan-

tage of being able to maintain a constant, high body temperature. This keeps the delicate machinery of the body processes
tuned in for top performance. It is not a property to be endan-
gered or discarded lightly. The temperature-controlling devices
are of vital importance and the possession of a thick, hairy,
insulating coat obviously plays a major role in preventing heat
loss. In intense sunlight it will also prevent over-heating and
damage to the skin from direct exposure to the sun's rays. If the
hair has to go, then clearly there must be a very powerful reason for abolishing it. With few exceptions this drastic step has
been taken only when mammals have launched themselves
into an entirely new medium. The flying mammals, the bats,
have been forced to denude their wings, but they have retained
their furriness elsewhere and can hardly be counted as naked
species. The burrowing mammals have in a few cases—the
naked mole rat, the aardvark and the armadillo, for example—
reduced their hairy covering. The aquatic mammals such as the
whales, dolphins, porpoises, dugongs, manatees and hip-
popotamuses have also gone naked as part of a general stream-
lining. But for all the more typical surface-dwelling mammals,
whether scampering about on the ground or clambering
around in the vegetation, a densely hairy hide is the basic rule.
Apart from those abnormally heavy giants, the rhinos and the
elephants (which have heating and cooling problems peculiar
to themselves), the naked ape stands alone, marked off by his
nudity from all the thousands of hairy, shaggy or furry land-
dwelling mammalian species.

At this point the zoologist is forced to the conclusion that
either he is dealing with a burrowing or an aquatic mammal,
or there is something very odd, indeed unique, about the evolutionary history of the naked ape.

Fighting
    . . . Having brought up the question of religion, it is perhaps
worthwhile taking a closer look at this strange pattern of animal
behaviour, before going on to deal with other aspects of the
aggressive activities of our species. It is not an easy subject to

deal with, but as zoologists we must do our best to observe what actually happens rather than listen to what is supposed to be happening. If we do this, we are forced to the conclusion that, in a behavioural sense, religious activities consist of the coming together of large groups of people to perform repeated and prolonged submissive displays to appease a dominant individual. The dominant individual concerned takes many forms in different cultures, but always has the common factor of immense power. Sometimes it takes the shape of an animal from another species, or an idealized version of it. Sometimes it is pictured more as a wise and elderly member of our own species. Sometimes it becomes more abstract and is referred to as simply as "the state," or in other such terms. The submissive responses to it may consist of closing the eyes, lowering the head, clasping the hands together in a begging gesture, kneeling, kissing the ground, or even extreme prostration, with the frequent accompaniment of wailing or chanting vocalizations. If these submissive actions are successful, the dominant individual is appeased. Because its powers are so great, the appeasement ceremonies have to be performed at regular and frequent intervals, to prevent its anger from rising again. The dominant individual is usually, but not always, referred to as a god.

Since none of these gods exist in a tangible form, why have they been invented? To find the answer to this we have to go right back to our ancestral origins. Before we evolved into co-operative hunters, we must have lived in social groups of the type seen today in other species of apes and monkeys. There, in typical cases, each group is dominated by a single male. He is the boss, the overlord, and every member of the group has to appease him or suffer the consequences. He is also most active in protecting the group from outside hazards and in settling squabbles between lesser members. The whole life of a member of such a group revolves around the dominant animal. His all-powerful role gives him a god-like status. Turning now to our immediate ancestors, it is clear that, with the growth of the co-operative spirit so vital for successful group hunting, the application of the dominant individual's authority had to be severely limited if he was to retain the active, as opposed to passive, loyalty of the other group members. They had to want to help him instead of simply fear him. He had to become more "one of them." The old-style monkey tyrant had to go, and in his place there arose a more tolerant, more co-operative naked ape leader. This step was essential for the new type of "mutual-aid" organization that was evolving, but it gave rise to a problem. The total dominance of the Number 1 member of the group having been replaced by a qualified dominance, he could no longer command unquestioning allegiance. This change in the order of things, vital as it was to the new social system, nevertheless left a gap. From our ancient background there remained a need for an all-powerful figure who could keep the group under control, and the vacancy was filled by the invention of a god. The influence of the invented god-figure could then operate as a force additional to the now more restricted influence of the group leader.

At first sight, it is surprising that religion has been so successful, but its extreme potency is simply a measure of the strength of our fundamental biological tendency, inherited directly from our monkey and ape ancestors, to submit ourselves to an all-powerful, dominant member of the group. Because of this, religion has proved immensely valuable as a device for aiding social cohesion, and it is doubtful whether our species could have progressed far without it, given the unique combination of circumstances of our evolutionary origins. It has led to a number of bizarre by-products, such as a belief in "another life" where we will at last meet up with the god figures. They were, for reasons already explained, unavoidably detained from joining us in the present life, but this omission can be corrected in an after-life. In order to facilitate this, all kinds of strange practices have been developed in connection with the disposal of our bodies when we die. If we are going to join our dominant overlords, we must be well prepared for the occasion and elaborate burial ceremonies must be performed.

Religion has also given rise to a great deal of unnecessary suffering and misery, wherever it has become over-formalized in its application, and whenever the professional "assistants" of the god figures have been unable to resist the temptation to borrow a little of his power and use it themselves. But despite its chequered history it is a feature of our social life that we cannot do without. Whenever it becomes unacceptable, it is quietly, or sometimes violently, rejected, but in no time at all it is back again in a new form, carefully disguised perhaps, but containing all the same old basic elements. We simply have to "believe in something." Only a common belief will cement us together and keep us under control. It could be argued that, on this basis, any belief will do, so long as it is powerful enough; but this is not strictly true. It must be impressive and it must be seen to be impressive. Our communal nature demands the performance of and participation in elaborate group ritual. . . .

Before we embarked on this religious discourse, we had been examining the nature of only one aspect of the organization of aggressiveness in our species, namely the group defense of a territory. But as I explained at the beginning of this chapter, the naked ape is an animal with three distinct social forms of aggression, and we must now consider the other two. They are the territorial defense of the family-unit within the larger group-unit, and the personal, individual maintenance of hierarchy positions.

The spatial defense of the home site of the family unit has remained with us through all our massive architectural advances. Even our largest buildings, when designed as living-quarters, are assiduously divided into repetitive units, one per family. There has been little or no architectural "division of labour." Even the introduction of communal eating or drinking buildings, such as restaurants and bars, has not eliminated the inclusion of dining-rooms in the family unit quarters. Despite all the other advances, the design of our cities and towns is still dominated by our ancient, naked-ape need to divide our groups up into small, discrete, family territories. Where houses have not yet been squashed up into blocks of flats, the defended area is carefully fenced, walled, or hedged off from its neighbors, and the demarcation lines are rigidly respected and adhered to, as in other territorial species.

One of the important features of the family territory is that it must be easily distinguished in some way from all the others. Its separate location gives it a uniqueness, of course, but this is not enough. Its shape and general appearance must make it stand out as an easily identifiable entity, so that it can become the "personalized" property of the family that lives there. This is something which seems obvious enough, but which has frequently been overlooked or ignored, either as a result of economic pressures, or the lack of biological awareness of architects. Endless rows of uniformly repeated, identical houses have been erected in cities and towns all over the world. In the case of blocks of flats the situation is even more acute. The psychological damage done to the territorialism of the families forced by architects, planners and builders to live under these conditions is incalculable. Fortunately, the families concerned can impose territorial uniqueness on their dwellings in other ways. The buildings themselves can be painted different colours. The gardens, where there are any, can be planted and landscaped in individual styles. The insides of the houses or flats can be decorated and filled with ornaments, bric-à-brac and personal belongings in profusion. This is usually explained as being done to make the place "look nice." In fact, it is the exact equivalent to another territorial species depositing its personal scent on a landmark near its den. When you put a name on a door, or hang a painting on a wall, you are, in dog or wolf terms, for example, simply cocking your leg on them and leaving your personal mark there. Obsessive "collecting" of specialized categories of objects occurs in certain individuals, who, for some reason, experience an abnormally strong need to define their home territories in this way.

Bearing this in mind, it is amusing to note the large number of cars that contain small mascots and other personal identification symbols, or to watch the business executive moving into a new office and immediately setting out on his desk his favourite personal pen-tray, paper-weight and perhaps a photograph of his wife. The motor-car and the business office are sub-territories, offshoots of his home base, and it is a great relief to be able to cock his leg on these as well, making them into more familiar, "owned" spaces.

This leaves us with the question of aggression in relation to the social dominance hierarchy. The individual, as opposed to the places he frequents, must also be defended. The social status must be maintained and, if possible improved, but it must be done cautiously, or he will jeopardize his co-operative contacts. This is where all the subtle aggressive and submissive signalling described earlier comes in to play. Group co-operativeness demands and gets a high degree of conformity in both dress and behaviour, but within the bounds of this conformity there is still great scope for hierarchy competitiveness. Because of these conflicting demands it reaches almost incredible degrees of sub-tlety. The exact form of the knotting of a tie, the precise arrange-ment of the exposed section of a breast-pocket handkerchief, minute distinctions in vocal accent, and other such seemingly trivial characteristics, take on a vital social significance in deter-mining the social standing of the individual. An experienced member of society can read them off at a glance. He would be totally at a loss to do so if suddenly jettisoned into the social hierarchy of New Guinea tribesmen, but in his own culture he is rapidly forced to become an expert. In themselves these tiny dif-ferences of dress and habit are utterly meaningless, but in rela-tion to the game of juggling for position and holding it in the dominance hierarchy they are all-important.

We did not evolve, of course, to live in huge conglomera-tions of thousands of individuals. Our behaviour is designed to operate in small tribal groups probably numbering well under a hundred individuals. In such situations every member of the tribe will be known personally to every other member, as is the case with other species of apes and monkeys today. In this type of social organization it is easy enough for the domi-nance hierarchy to work itself out and become stabilized, with only gradual changes as members become older and die. In a massive city community the situation is much more stressful. Every day exposes the urbanite to sudden contacts with countless strangers, a situation unheard-of in any other primate species. It is impossible to enter into personal hierarchy relationships with all of them, although this would be the natural tendency. Instead they are allowed to go scurrying by, undominated and undominating. In order to facilitate this lack of social contact, anti-touching behaviour patterns develop. This has already been mentioned when dealing with sexual behaviour, where one sex accidentally touches another, but it applies to more than simply the avoidance of sexual behaviour. It covers the whole range of social-relationship initiation. By carefully avoiding staring at one another, gesturing in one another's direction, signalling in any way, or making physical bodily contact, we manage to survive in an otherwise impossibly overstimulating social situation. If the no-touching rule is broken, we immediately apologize to make it clear that it was purely accidental.

Anti-contact behaviour enables us to keep our number of acquaintances down to the correct level for our species. We do this with remarkable consistency and uniformity. If you require confirmation, take the address or phone books of a hundred widely different types of city-dwellers and count up the number of personal acquaintances listed there. You will find that nearly all of them know well about the same number of individuals, and that this number approximates to what we would think of as a small tribal group. In other words, even in our social encounters we are obeying the basic biological rules of our ancient ancestors.

There will of course be exceptions to this rule—individuals who are professionally concerned with making large numbers of personal contacts, people with behaviour defects that make them abnormally shy or lonely, or people whose special psychological problems render them unable to obtain the expected social rewards from their friends and who try to compensate for this by frantic "socializing" in all directions. But these types account for only a small proportion of the town and city populations. All the rest happily go about their business in what seems to be a great seething mass of bodies, but which is in reality an incredibly complicated series of interlocking and overlapping tribal groups. How little, how very little, the naked ape has changed since his early, primitive days.

Questions

1. How does Morris describe the development of a god in the naked ape society? Who is this god and what is his purpose?
2. To what does Morris attribute the "surprising" success of religion? Why is there an afterlife?
3. Is Morris an evolutionist? Why? Where is God in his musings on the origin of *Homo sapiens*?

The Drugstore Curse

Maxine Hong Kingston

Maxine Hong Kingston is a Chinese-American author. In this selection from her book The Woman Warrior *Kingston relates a humorous childhood incident that illustrates the clash of worldviews and cultures. When a delivery boy makes a mistake with a prescription order, Maxine's Chinese mother considers it a crime which can only be rectified by Maxine's getting reparation candy from the druggist. It's an embarrassing situation for Maxine, who feels the "weight and immensity of things impossible to explain."*

We were working at the laundry when a delivery boy came from the Rexall drugstore around the corner. He had a pale blue box of pills, but nobody was sick. Reading the label we saw that it belonged to another Chinese family, Crazy Mary's family. "Not ours," said my father. He pointed out the name to the Delivery Ghost, who took the pills back. My mother muttered for an hour, and then her anger boiled over. "That ghost! That dead ghost! How dare he come to the wrong house?" She could not concentrate on her marking and pressing. "A mistake! Huh!" I was getting angry myself. She fumed. She made her press crash and hiss. "Revenge. We've got to avenge this wrong on our future, on our health, and on our lives. Nobody's going to sicken my children and get away with it." We brothers and sisters did not look at one another. She would do something awful, something embarrassing. She'd already been hinting that during the next eclipse we slam pot lids together to scare the frog from swallowing the moon. (The word for "eclipse" is *frog-swallowing-the-moon.*) When we had not banged lids at the last eclipse and the shadow kept receding anyway, she'd said, "The villagers must be banging and clanging very loudly back home in China."

("On the other side of the world, they aren't having an eclipse, Mama. That's just a shadow the earth makes when it comes between the moon and the sun."

"You're always believing what those Ghost Teachers tell you. Look at the size of the jaws!")

"Aha!" she yelled. "You! The biggest." She was pointing at me. "You go to the drugstore."

"What do you want me to buy, Mother?" I said.

"But nothing. Don't bring one cent. Go and make them stop the curse."

"I don't want to go. I don't know how to do that. There are no such things as curses. They'll think I'm crazy."

"If you don't go, I'm holding you responsible for bringing a plague on this family."

"What am I supposed to do when I get there?" I said, sullen, trapped. "Do I say, 'Your delivery boy made a wrong delivery'?"

"They know he made a wrong delivery. I want you to make them rectify their crime."

I felt sick already. She'd make me swing stinky censers around the counter, at the druggist, at the customers. Throw dog blood on the druggist. I couldn't stand her plans.

"You get reparation candy," she said. "You say, 'You have tainted my house with sick medicine and must remove the curse with sweetness.' He'll understand."

"He didn't do it on purpose. And no, he won't, Mother. They don't understand stuff like that. I won't be able to say it right. He'll call us beggars."

"You just translate." She searched me to make sure I wasn't hiding any money. I was sneaky and bad enough to buy the candy and come back pretending it was a free gift.

"Mymotherseztagimmesomecandy" I said to the druggist. Be cute and small. No one hurts the cute and small.

"What? Speak up. Speak English," he said, big in his white druggist coat.

"Tatatagimme somecandy."

The druggist leaned way over the counter and frowned. "Some free candy," I said. "Sample candy."

"We don't give sample candy, young lady," he said.

"My mother said you have to give us candy. She said that is the way the Chinese do it."

"What?"

"That is the way the Chinese do it."

"Do what?"

"Do things." I felt the weight and immensity of things impossible to explain to the druggist.

"Can I give you some money?" he asked.

"No, we want candy."

He reached into a jar and gave me a handful of lollipops. He gave us candy all year round, year after year, every time we went into the drugstore. When different druggists or clerks waited on us, they also gave us candy. They had talked us over. They gave us Halloween candy in December, Christmas candy around Valentine's day, candy hearts at Easter, and Easter eggs at Halloween. "See?" said our mother. "They understand. You kids just aren't very brave." But I knew they did not understand. They thought we were beggars without a home who lived in back of the laundry. They felt sorry for us. I did not eat their candy. I did not go inside the drugstore or walk past it unless my parents forced me to. Whenever we had a prescription filled, the druggist put candy in the medicine bag. This is what Chinese druggists normally do, except they give raisins. My mother thought she taught the Druggist Ghosts a lesson in good manners (which is the same word as "traditions").

Questions

1. Why does Maxine's mother want her to get some candy from the druggist? Why doesn't her mother realize that the delivery boy simply made an honest mistake?

2. What does she say or do that reveals her superstition?

3. How does Maxine feel about going to the drugstore for the reparation candy? Why do you think she refuses to eat the candy?
4. How do the druggists and clerks respond to Maxine's request for candy? Do you think they eventually understand this Chinese family? Why or why not?

Psalm 8

For the director of music. According to gittith. A psalm of David.

Psalm 8 is an expression of praise to the Creator God by a writer who is obviously overwhelmed by God's glory arrayed in the starry heavens. In the same breath he expresses wonder at God's condescending to the level of puny human beings and raising them up to rule in the created order.

O LORD, our Lord,
>how majestic is your name in all the earth!

You have set your glory
>above the heavens.
From the lips of children and infants
>you have ordained praise
because of your enemies,
>to silence the foe and the avenger.

When I consider your heavens,
>the work of your fingers,
the moon and the stars,
>which you have set in place,
what is man that you are mindful of him,
>the son of man that you care for him?
You made him a little lower than the heavenly beings
>and crowned him with glory and honor.

You made him ruler over the works of your hands;
>you put everything under his feet:
all flocks and herds,
>and the beasts of the field,

the birds of the air,
>and the fish of the sea,
>all that swim the paths of the seas.

O LORD, our Lord,
>how majestic is your name in all the earth!

Questions

1. What words describe the psalmist's attitude toward God? Toward creation? Toward himself?
2. Why does the writer portray humankind as separate ("ruler") from creation? What does this teach about our role as created beings?
3. Does Psalm 8 inspire confidence or despair? Why?

Preamble—Our World Belongs to God

The Preamble to "Our World Belongs to God" is a summary of the Christian worldview. It sketches the outline of what the Bible teaches concerning creation, the fall, redemption and a new creation. "Our World Belongs to God" is a confessional statement adopted by the Christian Reformed Church in 1986 to help its members apply their Christian faith to contemporary issues.

Preamble

1. As followers of Jesus Christ, [1]
   living in this world—
   which some seek to control,
   but which others view with despair— [2]
   we declare with joy and trust:
   Our world belongs to God! [3]

   [1] Ps. 103:19-22
   [2] Ps. 4:6
   [3] Ps. 24:1

2. From the beginning, [1]
   through all the crises of our times,
   until his kingdom fully comes, [2]
   God keeps covenant forever.
   Our world belongs to him! [3]
   God is King! Let the earth be glad!
   Christ is Victor; his rule has begun. Hallelujah!
   The Spirit is at work, renewing the creation. Praise the
   Lord!

   [1] Ps. 145
   [2] Rom. 11:33-36
   [3] Rev. 4-5

3. But rebel cries sound through the world: [1]
    some, crushed by failure
    or hardened by pain,
    give up on life and hope and God;
    others, shaken,
    but still hoping for human triumph, [2]
    work feverishly to realize their dreams. [3]
    As believers in God
    we join this struggle of the spirits,
    testing our times by the Spirit's sure Word.
    [1] Ps. 2
    [2] Eph. 6:10-18
    [3] 1 John 4

4. Our world has fallen into sin;
    but rebellion and sin can never dethrone God. [1]
    He does not abandon the work of his hand;
    the heavens still declare his glory.
    He preserves his world,
    sending seasons, sun, and rain, [2]
    upholding his creatures,
    renewing the earth,
    directing all things to their purpose.
    He promised a Savior;
    now the whole creation groans [3]
    in the birth pangs of a new creation.
    [1] Ps. 19
    [2] Acts 14:15-17
    [3] Rom. 8:18-25

5. God holds this world [1]
   in sovereign love.
   He kept his promise,
   sending Jesus into the world.
   He poured out his Spirit [2]
   and broadcast the news
   that sinners who repent and believe in Jesus [3]
   can live
   and breathe
   and move again
   as members of the family of God.

   [1] John 3:1-21
   [2] Acts 2
   [3] Acts 17:22-31

6. We rejoice in the goodness of God,
   renounce the works of darkness,
   and dedicate ourselves to holy living.
   As covenant partners,
   called to faithful obedience, [1]
   and set free for joyful praise,
   we offer our hearts and lives [2]
   to do God's work in his world. [3]
   With tempered impatience, eager to see injustice ended,
   we expect the Day of the Lord.
   And we are confident
   that the light which shines in the present darkness [4]
   will fill the earth when Christ appears.

   Come, Lord Jesus! [5]
   Our world belongs to you.

   [1] Mic. 6:8
   [2] Rom. 12:1-2
   [3] 2 Pet. 3
   [4] 1 Cor. 15
   [5] Rev. 22:20

Questions

1. This selection is a brief summary of the Christian world-view. In a word or two, what is the topic of each section?
2. What is the basis for the statements in this selection?
3. What feeling do you get from reading these statements? Do you feel uplifted and confident or confused and afraid? Why?

2

Common
Objections
to the
Christian Faith

Introductory Readings

Still Looking: Will Rob Find Faith?

Chris Lutes

This selection is an interview first published in Campus
Life *magazine. Rob is a high school student who raises several important questions about Christianity. The son of divorced parents, Rob has been very angry at God. He has become more accepting of Christianity, yet is not sure what it would take for him to believe that Christianity is true.*

As I stepped inside the house on Nantucket Circle Drive, I was immediately introduced to a tall, lanky guy wearing an "Epcot Center" T-shirt. His hair was brown and short, except for the "tail" that trailed down the back of his neck. His eye color was hidden by the brown tint of wire-rimmed glasses. So this was Rob.

Earlier that day, Tim had asked me to drop over at his house to meet this friend of his. "Rob isn't a Christian," Tim had said, "but he's searching hard—and I think he has a lot to say." Tim felt Rob would make a good interview for *Campus Life*. I wasn't convinced. I do a lots of interviews for the magazine and some turn into stories; many don't. I honestly wasn't expecting too much. And yet sometimes you meet somebody who causes you to do some serious thinking about what you believe, what you really hold as true. For me that somebody became Rob.

Seated on the couch in Tim's living room Rob was visibly nervous. He fiddled self-consciously, and when he spoke his voice quivered slightly. As I set up my tape recorder, I smiled, joked a bit, trying to make him feel relaxed and comfortable.

After a couple of minutes of light conversation, I began to question Rob about his background and experiences. Soon I discovered that he'd been "baptized" as a baby; he'd also received some "religious instruction" in a pre-school he once attended. Eventually, though, his neat, simple world of childhood faith began to slip away. "I became," he explained, "probably more anti-church than anything else.

"I turned against religion," Rob said with a tinge of emotion, "because I couldn't understand a lot of the things that were happening to me and to my family. I couldn't really put it together. There was supposed to be this God somewhere up there in control of it all, and yet my family was falling apart."

He sat for a moment, silent. Then leaning forward, he clasped his hands together and continued, explaining that his parents had divorced when he was 7. Rob moved many times, living for a while with his mother, for a while with his father. There had been many painful separations. And financial struggles. Why was his family, why was he, being put through this hell?

"I couldn't help thinking," said Rob, "that if God was supposed to be so great, then why was he letting this happen to me? Why was he allowing this to happen to my family?" Rob couldn't find answers, so, as he put it, "I chose not to believe in him."

As Rob moved out of childhood and into his junior-high and early high-school years, his anger toward God expressed itself in arguments with Christian friends about "the Bible's silly myths." He would taunt his friends with questions like, "Can a man really live to be over 900 years?" "Why would any intelligent person believe that a fish would swallow and then spit out a living man?" "What about a boat full of *all* the world's animals?" And so on.

Then there were the nagging, and more serious, questions about pain, suffering and evil; the so-called religious war in Ireland; the oppression in South Africa; Ethiopia's starving millions. *And,* I thought as I listened to him, *there's also the long-lasting, unresolved hurt over his parents' divorce.* In Rob's mind, God was to blame for all of this. Along with the doubt and cynicism, Rob had grown very lonely.

During his junior year, amid all the inner confusion and family turmoil, Rob started attending a Christian club at his high school. He wasn't clear about why he decided to go. "But," he said, "I've always had trouble making friends and I thought this might be a good way to meet some people—they all seemed friendly enough." One of Rob's new friends was Tim, the club's off-campus, adult leader. Through Tim's influence, Rob finally started seeing some things about Christianity (and Christians) he could appreciate.

"I liked a lot of the values I saw in these people. The Christian idea of 'doing unto others as you would have others do unto you' seemed to be a good way to live your life. Their definition of 'love' made sense to me too. And it seemed like these Christians had a firm grasp of what it meant to be a real friend. Tim and his wife, Sandy, have been very good to me too."

And yet, Rob's experiences with Christians have not all been positive.

"I have a problem with some Christians I know, because they seem a bit self-righteous, even a little two-faced. I had this one friend and we were very, very close. His parents are devout Christians and so is he. And yet they seem obsessed with their wealth. If something comes into their lives that disturbs their social standing or if financial difficulties come along, it is time for immediate worry or concern. It seems to me that they put material things above everything else."

I asked him if he saw this as an obstacle to becoming a Christian.

"I used to. But I can deal with it now. I just see it as a deficiency in the person, not as a flaw in the Christian faith."

His answer surprised me, and I let him know that. He had taken an interesting step. He had decided not to fault Christianity for the mistakes or wrong-doings of certain Christians.

"I helps that I have come in contact with some Christians who are strong in their faith," Rob explained, "who aren't perfect, and yet who try to live by their Christian beliefs. As for the others, I assume the problem is not the Christian faith itself, but rather, the shortcomings of people who, for one reason or another, are weak in their faith."

I wondered, then, were there issues about Christianity that *continued* to bother him?

"Well, here's something that I guess could be seen as a 'deficiency' in people and not Christianity, and yet it really does bother me. A lot of Christians seem so full of contempt and dislike, even hate, for people who don't agree with them. I visited this church awhile back and attended the high-school Sunday school class. The entire class got into a lengthy discussion about 'Moonies.' They kept carrying on about how bad these people were."

I was curious to know what bothered Rob the most: Was it the way in which these Christians were putting down a religious sect? Or was he bothered more by the fact that they believed Christianity to be the only way to God?

"I don't mind Christianity saying that it's the only way to God. As far as I'm concerned, a religion can claim that it is right. But to be so unkind and hard on a group of people they probably know very little about—that seemed wrong."

So what would it take to make Christianity seem "true" for Rob?

"I'm not really sure. A lot of my questions are being answered—Tim has been a big help there. But what keeps gnawing at me is this whole problem of justice. In my mind,

God doesn't seem very fair. I guess if I picked up the paper tomorrow and the headlines read: 'All Wars Have Stopped' and 'All Hunger Has Been Solved'—I would have no other choice than to believe. Now I'm not saying that I want to be put in a situation where I have no choice in the matter. To be honest with you, I'm not sure what it would take to cause me to believe."

I decided to press this point a little further. I explained that some people are dabblers; they like to try this and try that—but really aren't serious about their pursuits. They like to search, but they aren't too interested in finding. Before I finished making my point, however, Rob interrupted me.

"It's true that I have spent some time looking into various beliefs," Rob said. "I have, for instance, attended a Buddhist temple, and during my sophomore year I was even into meditation. I've tried a few things. And I think if someone right now would look at me and look at my past four years, they would say that I'm a 'dabbler.' But what I'm really doing is trying to find out what's right for me. So far, Christianity has been the belief I've stuck with the longest. I've been looking into it for over a year now."

I wondered, then, in view of all this, what Rob thought about Jesus Christ. Who is he, and what part does he play in the search?

"I know the Church says that Jesus was the Son of God, and that he was God's way of cleaning up our messed up lives and of helping us to become united with God. Right now, however, I see him as a very intelligent, very good person who was interested in the welfare and future of individuals and of humanity in general. Quite honestly, if he were on earth today, I would hope that he'd be someone like Tim. Obviously, if he were here today, he wouldn't have the flaws that Tim and other Christians have. Yet all the good I see in Tim, all the good I see in other Christian people, I believe I'd see in him."

Questions

1. What are some of Rob's objections to Christianity?
2. What other religious "dabbling" has Rob engaged in?
3. Where did Rob's dissatisfaction with Christianity begin? How has he felt about religion through the years?
4. What role has Tim played in Rob's search? Do you think Tim's role has been important? Why or why not?

1.) Some Christians are not who they say they are. Some are holier than thou. Christianity didn't seem to answer why all of the hurt in the world.

2.) T.M., Buddhism

3.) It began with his parents being separated. He has been very untrusting yet is seeking answers to the question why?

4.) Tim was an example onto Jesus Christ. His life was a standard to offered Rob hope.

Why We Believe

Paul Little

Before his death in 1975, Paul Little was a popular author and campus speaker for InterVarsity Christian Fellowship. His book How to Give Away Your Faith *is an excellent resource for Christians who desire help and encouragement in their witness. This selection is excerpted from that book. Little says that it's not good enough to know* what *you believe as a Christian; you must also know* why *you believe it. He says that while a well-reasoned testimony alone won't convert anybody, God can use our words "as an instrument to bring someone to faith in Jesus Christ."*

In our time it's not enough to know what we believe as Christians; we must also know why we believe it. All Christians should be able to defend their faith. We're clearly instructed about this spiritual responsibility in 1 Peter 3:15: "In your hearts set apart Christ as Lord. Always be prepared to give an answer to everyone who asks you to give the reason for the hope you have. But do this with gentleness and respect."

This command is not optional and there are good, practical reasons for it. First, for the sake of our own conviction about the truth, we should have an answer ready. Unless we are fully persuaded in our own minds that Jesus Christ is the truth, we will never effectively communicate the gospel to someone else. Moreover our own spiritual lives will soon become impoverished. We cannot drive ourselves to do with our wills something about which we are not intellectually convinced; the result is emotional collapse. We ourselves must be convinced of the truth.

Second, we have a responsibility to help thoughtful non-Christians deal with their honest questions about Christianity.

If we are constantly silenced by non-Christians' questions, we are confirming their reasons for unbelief.

I'm not suggesting we should stop witnessing about Jesus Christ if we don't have all the answers. We can always point to our own experience, as did one courageous man Jesus healed. In John 9, when he was asked questions he couldn't answer, he told his critics simply, "One thing I do know. I was blind but now I see!" (v. 25). When we don't know the answers we can always stand squarely on what we *do* know: Jesus Christ has changed our lives. However, this should not be our only recourse. We are responsible for mastering the answers to repeatedly asked questions.

Two Harmful Attitudes

In considering and answering the questions non-Christians ask, we need to avoid two opposite but equally harmful attitudes. The first is basically an anti-intellectual attitude. Some people assert, "You don't have to bother with human wisdom. Don't even try to think out Christianity." They imply that it's wrong to try to work ideas through.

Or you'll hear, "Don't get sidetracked by people's questions. Just preach the simple gospel." The tragic result of accepting such a view is that many thinking non-Christians conclude from our behavior that their honest questions have no answers. And we sometimes begin to wonder ourselves whether or not we have the truth: if we faced the facts as they really are, would our faith hold water? The anti-intellectual attitude is usually a dead-end street for both the non-Christian and for us.

Second, we must guard against a naive reliance on the answers we have, as though answers themselves will bring people to Jesus Christ. Sometimes we think that any explanation that makes sense to us and has helped a few others is a magic wand. We think we'll go out and wow people with it, so they'll have no choice except to believe. Of course, we're naive in thinking this, for we've already noted that no one calls Jesus Lord except by the Holy Spirit. Unless the Holy Spirit illumines people's minds to see the truth as truth, unless he bends their proud wills to submit to the authority of Jesus Christ, no words of ours will penetrate. But in the hands of God an intelligent answer to their questions may well be the instrument that opens their hearts and minds to the gospel.

There is no doubt we are in a spiritual warfare involving ourselves and the questioners. Paul explained the reason that people do not believe: "The god of this age has blinded the minds of unbelievers, so that they cannot see the light of the gospel of the glory of Christ" (2 Corinthians 4:4). Information cannot bring them to the truth unless a supernatural work also occurs to enlighten them. Often God and the Holy Spirit will use a presentation of information as an instrument to bring someone to faith in Jesus Christ.

Questions

1. According to Little, why should Christians be able to defend their faith? How important is it to relate our own experience of faith?

2. Read 1 Peter 3:15. Write the verse in your own words. To whom is this verse directed? What is its message for you?

Giving Reasons for Our Faith

Rebecca Manley Pippert

This essay is from Rebecca Manley Pippert's practical book on evangelism Out of the Saltshaker and Into the World. *Pippert notes that Christians do not have absolute proof for their beliefs, but they do have sufficient evidence. When used with apologetic skill and with a focus on Jesus Christ, such evidence can be very persuasive to a serious seeker.*

Let's say Ralph Nader had a conversion experience. Now for Nader facts are everything. But what if he suddenly declared to the public, "I had this incredible experience last week while looking at my tulip patch. I'm now a believer. And I get up early every morning and bow down and worship the tulip seeds"?

I bet many people would say, "Oh, wow, that's really beautiful, Ralph. You know, whatever turns you on is okay. I mean as long as it works for you then that's great." Only a few would say, "How do you know it's true? How do you know you're not creating your own little world and calling it 'reality'?" We would check his facts in any other area but this one, because in religion, we are told, as long as we are sincere then it is true enough.

But something is wrong here. Hitler was sincere, drug addicts are sincere, the followers of the People's Temple in Jonestown were sincere. Sincerity just cannot be an adequate basis for determining truth. Our concept of truth in religion has been so drastically reduced that something is true if it makes us feel good or comes from sincere motives. But as the adage goes, we need more than sincerity because we can be so sincerely wrong!

What we need is a faith that corresponds to the reality around us, that makes sense out of our world, that is internally consistent and hangs together. As Christians we do not have absolute proof for our belief in Jesus. There is in fact no absolute proof for any ultimate proposition, whether Christian or Buddhist or atheist or whatever. But the God of the Bible does not call us to leap in the dark; he does not require faith without evidence, for that is mere superstition.

I used to feel frustrated as an agnostic asking Christians truth questions when they always answered, "It's just this feeling in my heart."

"But I need something for my head too!" I would respond. And to my delight I found God offered both. He gives us the subjective experience of knowing him and objective evidence to act upon. It is not evidence that overwhelms us or answers every question, but it is evidence that is sufficient.

To further sharpen the effectiveness of our conversations, we can learn to employ some basic apologetic skills. In the process this will build our own confidence in the truth of Christianity. I will mention briefly three areas of evidence: historical, philosophical and personal.

Historical Evidence

People often respond very sentimentally to my faith. They say, "I think it's beautiful what your faith does for you. It's really your thing. I mean it's not my thing, but it's so nice for you."

To which I say, "But do you think it's true?"

They usually say no, and so I often continue the conversation in one of two ways.

One way is to say, "How can a lie be beautiful? Either I am right or else hopelessly deceived. If I am wrong, then I have stacked my entire life on falsehood. If I'm deceived, then it's ugly, not beautiful."

Another way is to say, "Despite your thoughtfulness in saying my faith is valid for me because it gives me such a warm feeling, all of the tenderest feelings in the world cannot make a man rise from the dead. Either Jesus did or did not, quite apart from my feelings on the subject. And one of the most attested facts in history is that his tomb was empty. The government turned Jerusalem upside down trying to find the corpse. Either Jesus resurrected or there must be an explanation of what happened to his corpse. But neither conclusion depends on my warm glow to make it true. Jesus isn't true just because he makes me feel good."

This moves us into the arena of historical evidences. Questions such as, How do you know the Bible is historically trustworthy? Was Jesus merely a good teacher? How do you know he was resurrected? Did Jesus even exist? Why Christianity and not other religions? These questions all require evidence. A variety of books in this area can give us surer footing. The questions non-Christians ask are remarkably similar. It would be helpful to have index cards with the problem stated at the top—"Evidence for the Resurrection"—-and the basic arguments listed below. Paul Little's *Know Why You Believe* is structured around twelve questions non-Christians most frequently ask. That would be a good place to start learning how they may best be answered.

Philosophical Evidence

Some of the philosophical questions that Christians need to know how to answer are, How could a good God allow evil or hell? Are people basically good but simply misinformed and will improve with the proper controls? Are we merely machines, matter-in-motion? How can we talk of absolutes (that something is "good" or "unjust") when everything is relative or merely by chance?

There are many excellent books that deal with these issues in depth. Here I want to suggest some basic guidelines. Being able to put new ideas or old arguments into proper categories can be helpful. Even recognizing that one question requires historical evidence while another requires philosophical is a start. When someone exposes a thought or system you are unfamiliar with, do not get bogged down in a myriad of details. You need not feel intimidated by a system of thought you do not know. It is impossible to read everything. Try to get at the heart of their system, and that will help you (and probably them) categorize it and understand it properly.

Listen carefully and sympathetically as they articulate their beliefs. Get their views on several issues. See if you can get to the core of their beliefs by asking a few basic questions. It is surprising how relatively few basic answers there are to ultimate questions. The details of system may differ, but most ideas can be put into a few slots. Here are some examples:

1. *The basic nature of the world.* Do people or their arguments begin from the premise that there is no God, that we started from nothing or from matter only? Or if they believe in God, what kind of God is it (personal or impersonal, finite or infinite, involved with human affairs or aloof)?

Discovering whether they begin from a naturalistic premise or a supernatural one will determine a great deal. For example, if they do not believe in God and maintain that the universe is closed, mechanistic and impersonal, it would be impossible for them to believe in biblical miracles. If they do not believe in the supernatural, then it is pointless to keep arguing about something that their system could never accommodate. We should point out to them, however, that it is utterly consistent for us to acknowledge the possibility of miracles because our system allows for the supernatural. So instead of banging away at the possibility of miracles, we might ask that since they deny the existence of God and the existence of absolute truths, are they able to live consistently with such beliefs?

2. *Morality.* Closely related to the question of whether God exists—and if so, what kind of God it is—is the issue of ultimate morality. If a God who is interested in matters of ethics does not exist, then there may be no basis outside ourselves for determining what is right and wrong. I know many students who think in exactly that way, and they claim to be able to live consistently with that notion.

They advocate "free love," for example, because, since there is no absolute standard of morality, sexual ethics is

reduced to a question of taste and preference. Nonetheless—
and this is the point—those same students are *rigid moralists* in
opposing racial prejudice, child brutality, war and so forth.
And why are they against such things? "Because they are
wrong, categorically and universally!" they retort.

But we cannot have it both ways. We must play by the
same rules on different issues. We can legitimately and forcefully challenge them, "If you say there is no such thing as
morality in absolute terms, then child abuse is not evil, it just
may not happen to be your thing. And if you find you are not
able to practice your premises with much consistency, then you
need to re-examine your premises." Most people's response to
evil is one of horror. When we read of the mass suicides in
Jonestown, our immediate response is "That is wrong! It is
evil!" or when we hear of abject poverty or senseless torture,
we say, "That is unfair, unjust!" Or conversely, when we see a
masterpiece, we say, "It is beautiful." In all this we are seeing
people responding to the fact that they are made in the image
of God—a good God, a God of beauty.

Our feelings of justice, of goodness, of beauty, stem from
the God who enshrines these very qualities and who made us
like himself. As C. S. Lewis says, to call a line crooked still
implies we know what a straight line is. To protest evil, as the
Marxists do, tells us they have a strong sense of what is right,
and they are angry to see it violated. So we must ask, Where
do our feelings of right and wrong, evil and good, come from?
What is the origin of these qualities? Where did our culture
derive these strong beliefs?

Challenging our non-Christian friends on whether they live
consistently by their own self-acknowledged principles is an
effective way of casting doubt on their present beliefs. Francis
Schaeffer has explained much about this in *The God Who Is There*.
So if you are naturally drawn to thinking or find you need help
in straightening out the issues, reading that book is a good next
step. You may find yourself going back again and again to it and
other books like Os Guiness's *In Two Minds,* or James Sire's *The
Universe Next Door* or C. S. Lewis's *Mere Christianity* and *Miracles*.

The point is that the Christian world view gives solid, intellectually profound answers to the very questions most people ask when they find their own answers are inadequate.

3. *Human nature.* Some people think a human being is only a set of chemicals, a piece of protoplasm. That is a valid philosophical position. But we may ask, Can they live that way?

I had a biology professor who stated the first day of class, "Man is merely a fortuitous concourse of atoms, a meaningless piece of protoplasm in an absurd world." We were taught that having deep regard for random products of the universe where chance is king was inconsistent. Some time later he told our class in despair that his thirteen-year-old daughter had run away to live with an older man. "She will be deeply wounded. She will scar, and I can't do anything to help. I must sit back and watch a tragedy," he said grimly.

I raised my hand and said, quietly, that according to his system protoplasm could not scar.

His answer was devastating. "Touché. I could never regard my daughter as a set of chemicals, never. I can't take my beliefs that far. Class dismissed."

Because we are made in the image of God, no matter how hard we try, we can never escape reacting to the world at some point, like God has made us. Sooner or later we will expose our God image. And when that point comes for the people God has given us to know, we must lovingly challenge them to quit escaping reality and live as they were created to be—children of God.

4. *The fundamental problem in the world and how we deal with it.* Everyone from physicists to poets agree that something is wrong with the world. Philosophies, ideologies or explanations of the life process usually place the blame either on external circumstances or on individual decisions and actions. If they see the source as external, then they usually say the system needs changing. For example, an individual is not bad or selfish, he has just developed poor habits; he is a victim of an externally imposed evil. Whether the evil culprit is the capitalistic economic superstructure as Marx suggested or the environment as

behavioral determinist B. F. Skinner theorizes, the focus of blame is outward not inward. The other alternative sees the problem as derived from some kind of internal chaos. Christianity says evil has permeated both levels and we must fight evil at both levels. But the *source* of evil is internal (Mk. 7:14-22).

When we meet optimistic humanists who believe people are basically good, we must agree first. One pillar of our understanding of humanity is that God declared his creation *good* (Gen. 1). Our ability to respond with compassion, to be moved by the beauty of a Da Vinci painting or the soaring Austrian Alps stems from the fact that we were created with wondrously good qualities. But we are not naive about the other aspect of our humanness—our sinfulness. The Bible deals utterly realistically with both sides of us. We are not intrinsically cruel, God did not make us evil. But he made us free. And we rebelled. We are not now what we were created to be. By our own decision we became abnormal when we chose not to be in relationship to God (Gen. 3).

So when optimists say that people are basically good but just need a bit more education or the right controls, we must ask them, "How do you account for two world wars? For rampant bigotry that still exists in our age of enlightenment? How do we write off the atrocities of the Hitler era or of the People's Temple in Guyana? How do we explain Watergate adequately?" My husband, who was principal UPI reporter on Watergate, says, "Watergate provided us a refresher course in basic theology; it reminded us of the reality of evil in a relativistic era. Christians above all others should have understood a basic cause of Watergate—the lure of power, to which so many White House aides succumbed—because it was one of the first temptations with which Jesus was confronted. But it also reminded us of the ever-present possibility of redemption and renewal. Lives were changed for good because of Watergate."

We must not be naive about the reality of evil. Nor can we afford to fail putting tough questions to advocates of the human potentials movement. No one should know or understand better the heights to which humans can climb or the depths to which we can succumb than a Christian. Therefore we must force the world to take both human goodness and human evil with the utmost seriousness. And when their analysis of our dilemma is shallow or their solution merely a Band-Aid approach, we must help them see that.

I was sitting next to a beautiful black law student on a bus to Salem, Oregon. We were discussing our heroes when she told me Karl Marx was her hero. When I asked why, she said, "Because of his passionate regard for the oppressed."

"I agree with that concern," I responded, "but what is Marx's view of the universe? For example, I know he holds no belief in God."

"Oh, yes," she replied, "Marx is very intelligent. He sees the universe as godless, and we have meaning only in a corporate sense of class. We are not significant as individuals."

"Yet you admire his regard for the oppressed even though they are ultimately insignificant. It seems strange to value them so highly when they are random products of a universe. Why not manipulate them as you please?" I asked.

"I couldn't do that. I guess if my natural response is to feel people are significant then I need a philosophic system that says the same thing," she astutely observed. "But I believe we are basically good. If we could live in a classless society, we would be free of the things that weigh us down. I really think on the basis of economic determinism we will be saved."

"Do you really believe if we lived in the ideal Marxist society our problem would be voted out?" I asked.

"Absolutely," she said.

I took a deep breath and said, "Listen. I know a guy. He is one of the worst racists I have ever met. If he lived with you for fifty years in your classless society, every time he saw you he'd still think 'nigger.' How can Marx wipe out the ugliness and hatred of a bigot?"

She turned away from me, her eyes glaring, and, looking out the window she said, "Right on. We've been trying to change that for centuries. And all of the rules and laws in the world can't change you. The laws curb behavior, they can force you to treat me justly, but they can't make you love me."

I knew I had struck a raw nerve but I felt I had to. Anyone who has suffered as blacks have in this society must know that an external change does not mean an internal change. I said, "You tell me you know people are significant, and you need a system that says so. Now you're saying that the real evil comes from within us. For external rules or laws can curb but not transform behavior. So you need a system that regards evil as internal and a solution that transforms radically not curbs superficially. Right?"

"Yeah, well it'll take more than a human attempt to change us that much. But we need it," she said.

"I couldn't agree more. In fact that's the very kind of system I've found," I said.

"Really? Hey, what revolution are you into?"

When I told her I followed Jesus, I think I had better not quote her exact words of response! But after she recovered from her shock she asked me how I knew it was true. For the rest of our trip she asked me to defend Christianity. She listened intently, and when we arrived she said, "I'd like to get together again. And there's something you're not going to believe. When I went home this weekend my younger sister came to see me, too. Then she told me she'd become a Christian. I told her it was anti-intellectual and unsubstantiated. In a furor I packed my bags, walked out saying I never wanted to discuss it again, got on the bus and sat down next to you."

We do indeed worship the Hound of Heaven.

Personal Evidence

Another effective form of evidence is what God has done in our own lives. The world hungers—perhaps without even knowing it—for examples of evidence in people's lives. They want to know if God works. Has he brought you a feeling of self-esteem? Does God make a difference in a marriage and in raising children?

Earl Palmer said once that perhaps the best testimony a Christian couple can give today is a reasonably good marriage.

We who are married do not have to pretend we are living as Barbie Dolls on a wedding cake. We have struggles, and dashed expectations too. But if we offer the world a model of a reasonably good marriage, a reasonably good church, a reasonably good college fellowship, it will have radicalizing effects on the world. We need to tell others what prayers we see answered, what things God is doing. We must communicate his aliveness!

Every Christian has a personal story to tell. Each of you who reads this book is unique. God has called you to be a very specific, very special person, and your story, your life is a testimony to God's goodness, his grace, his forgiveness. So share who you are with people. Let them know you have struggles but that Jesus has made a difference.

I have told many stories in this book—some of which have surprised me even more than the others involved. The changes God has wrought in people always amaze me. But he has wrought good works in you too. Don't be afraid to tell people who you are—and who you were before you met Christ.

True, some people only testify to themselves. "Once I was a louse. Now I'm great." God sometimes drops out of the testimony altogether. Or all of their witness is simply personal—what God has done for them. "I know he lives, because he lives within my heart." We must direct people's attention outward to God in Christ loving and reconciling the world to himself by the death of his Son on the cross. But the subjective dimension is equally real and, when balanced by the objective and historical, is a powerful witness to who God really is.

Whether we begin with historical, philosophical or personal evidence, we want to direct attention to Jesus. We want them to examine him and his claims by what they see in our lives and our minds. We need to offer the world models of "head-and-heart" Christianity.

Questions

1. What are three types of evidence that can support a Christian testimony? Is one more important than the others? How do they differ?
2. What is philosophical evidence? What four areas of belief does philosophical evidence commonly cover?
3. Why is personal evidence a valid approach for defending your faith? What caution should be heeded when using personal evidence?
4. What authors and resources does Pippert recommend for each area of evidence?

How Can I Believe in Such an Exclusive Religion?

Why I'm Not a Christian: A Report

Robert Kachur

If it is important that we know what and why we believe, it is also imperative that Christians prepare to defend their faith by seeing it through the eyes of non-Christians. To obtain the non-Christian viewpoint, a student poll was conducted on three university campuses. The poll showed that students frequently claimed that Christianity was too exclusive. This objection was the second most common response in the survey.

Effective campus evangelism requires directly addressing the objections of unbelieving students and faculty. But what are these objections? If the good news is so good, why do most college students decide the gospel isn't for them?

The best way to answer these questions, the editors of U magazine decided, was simply to ask people. So we set out for three very different campuses: Northern Illinois University, a four-year state school; College of DuPage, a two-year commuter school; and Northwestern University, a private four-year "Big Ten" school. At each campus we set up a booth and offered students a free Coke (New, Classic, Diet or Cherry) if they would complete a brief, anonymous survey about religious faith, Christianity in particular.

Our goal wasn't to come away with statistics—we simply wanted students to tell us straight out how they perceive Christianity. Whether our perceptions are irrational, mistaken or right on, we all tend to base our decisions on them; we live as if our perceptions, right or wrong, tell the whole story. (For instance, a number of students said they shunned Christianity because of representative Christians like Jerry Falwell; Mother Teresa wasn't mentioned once.) If Christians desire to share their faith meaningfully, they must first ask, How do students perceive Christianity? How can we break through people's negative perceptions?

The results of our survey? Classic Coke whipped New Coke, with Cherry Coke coming in a close second. But more importantly, students identified several key factors that kept them from becoming Christians. . . .

Too Exclusive

Q. Why doesn't Christianity appeal to you?

A. I believe all religions are valid. God doesn't care how we worship as long as we are moral and love our neighbors.

We'd been standing in the rain at Northern Illinois for about an hour giving out wet Cokes when Joseph and his friend walked up to fill out surveys. As they leaned against a nearby wall to fill them out, Joseph began muttering. Finally he turned to us incredulously and blurted, "What do you mean 'Why doesn't Christianity appeal to me?' You can't jam your whole body into one way of thinking!" On paper he added: "There are too many people who see the world differently to limit yourself."

Joseph wasn't alone. Christianity's exclusivity proved to be the second most common reason students gave for not becoming Christians. Significantly, many who objected to Christianity's claim to be the only way to God seemed to associate Christianity's exclusivity with Christians who exclude or look down on others.

- *Buddhist journalism major:* "I don't like the way some Christians look down on other religions, especially Eastern philosophy. My religion is just as valid as theirs."
- *Senior political science major:* "I am Jewish. I am right in my beliefs. Someone else is Christian—they too are right! Why can't this seemingly illogical yet true statement just be accepted once and for all?!?"
- *Junior art history major:* "It seems that God would not exclude over half the world because they didn't accept Jesus."
- *Sophomore theater major:* "God's not so specific. Christianity is one of many plausible ways to a spiritual end."
- *Sophomore nutrition major:* "Any religion is good. You shouldn't be prejudiced about religion."
- *Psychology grad student:* "I know many Christians who are very intolerant of other beliefs—Protestants who don't like Catholics, Catholics who hate Jews, etc. There's one God and we all worship him in our own way."
- *Sophomore Asian studies major:* "Is Islam not also a religion worshiping the same God as Christians? There should be no sects."
- *Senior English major:* "Christianity's cool for others, but not my choice."
- *Freshman English major:* "You've got to be nuts to go through life believing that this is the only way."

At first students seemed to fall into three categories: Christians who believe Christ is the only way to God, non-Christians who believe there are many ways to God, and non-Christians who don't believe in or are indifferent to God. But a surprising number of those who checked "Christianity's too exclusive" also identified themselves as Christians who "try to apply the principles of (their) faith to everyday life." Interestingly, many of these folks had been going to church all their lives. How can students who seem to be committed Christians—like the practicing Roman Catholic of ten years who "enjoys talking to God"—also think Christianity's too exclusive?

Surveys, like people, can be tough to figure out. What's going through the mind of the sophomore who thinks both that "there's too much suffering in the world to believe in a loving God" and that people need Christianity because "the world's too tough to try and go it alone"? What about the theater major who doesn't know if she believes in God but sees herself remaining committed to the Protestant church for a long time? Or the two nursing students who'd been involved in the church for over fifteen years but checked "I don't really know much about Christianity"?

It's hard to say. People's perceptions stem from a variety of experiences. We don't always know how they fit together.

Questions

1. Why was the poll conducted? What information was it intended to reveal?
2. Why is it important to know what other people think concerning Christianity? What does that knowledge do for your own belief?
3. Do you believe Christianity is too exclusive? Do you think some of the objections have a degree of validity? Which ones and why?
4. How difficult is it to separate the objection from the person who holds it? What attitude traps do Christians sometimes fall into when they are faced with people who hold different views?

No Escape

R.C. Sproul

Theologian R. C. Sproul tells of one of the most humiliating experiences of his life. As a college student he was asked by a professor who was openly hostile to Christianity, "Do you believe that Jesus Christ is the only way to God?" When he answered in the affirmative, the professor's fury broke loose. She later apologized, yet raised the question of whether a person could believe in a God who allows only one way to himself.

One of the most embarrassing moments I ever experienced came in a freshman English class in college. It was a time of painful public humiliation. The professor was a former war correspondent who was outwardly hostile to Christianity. In the middle of a class she looked at me and said, "Mr. Sproul, do you believe that Jesus Christ is the only way to God?" I gasped as I felt the weight of her question and knew that every eye in the room was on me. My mind raced for a way to escape my dilemma. I knew that if I said yes people would be angry. At the same time, I knew that if I said no I would be betraying Christ. Finally, I mumbled almost inaudibly, "Yes, I do." The teacher responded with unmitigated fury. She said in front of the whole class, "That's the most narrow-minded, bigoted, and arrogant statement I have ever heard. You must be a supreme egotist to believe that your way of religion is the only way." I made no reply but slouched rather meekly in my chair.

After the class was dismissed, I went to speak with my teacher privately. In the conversation I tried to explain to her why I believed that Christ was the only way. I asked her if she thought that it was at least theoretically possible that Christ be one way to God. She allowed the possibility. I asked if she thought it were possible that without being narrow-minded or bigoted a person could come to the belief that Jesus was God. Though she did not believe in the deity of Christ, she recognized that people could, in fact, believe that without being bigoted. Then I explained to her that the reason I believed that Christ was the only way to God is because Christ Himself taught that. I reminded her that Jesus said, "I am the way, and the truth, and the life; no one comes to the Father, but by me" (John 14:6). I also pointed out that the New Testament refers to Christ as the "only begotten" of the Father, and that "there is no other name under heaven through which men must be saved" (see Acts 4:12). I said to her, "Can you see that I am torn between loyalty to Christ and the modern spirit of pluralism?" I said, "Do you see that it is possible for me to believe in the uniqueness of Christ because He taught it? If I believed that Christ was the only way because I believe that my way must be the only way because it is my way, that would be an act of arrogance and egotism." She finally acknowledged that it was possible for someone to believe in the uniqueness of Christ without being arrogant and apologized sincerely to me. However, she went on to raise a more serious question than the question of my arrogance. She said, "How can you believe in a God who only allows one way to Himself? Isn't it narrow-minded of God to restrict redemption to one Saviour and one faith?"

Aren't All Religions Basically the Same?

In the final analysis this is the issue that must be faced: Is God so narrow-minded that He provides only one way of redemption?

Questions

1. What was the professor's basic complaint about Christianity? Why did she call Christianity narrow-minded? What does arrogance have to do with it?

2. How did Sproul handle himself? How did he defend his faith? What techniques did he use? How did he use Scripture?

Is Jesus the Only Way?

Darrell Johnson

The Campus Evangelism Handbook *was written to help
students witness for Christ. This selection is excerpted from
that book. Johnson says that the biblical claim that Jesus is
the only way to salvation has caused the "scandal of particularity" for much of the world. But there are two good reasons
to believe what the Bible says about Jesus: no one else said
what Jesus said, and no one else did what Jesus did. This
should be enough to wipe away any fear you feel in witnessing for Jesus.*

Why is it that we disciples of Jesus Christ find it so difficult
to name his name in our world? We freely share our feelings
about the Middle Eastern struggle, the latest film or the way
the president handles the economy. We can even talk to others
about our latest romance. But when it comes to talking to others about Jesus, we hold back. Why? One word: *fear.* We fear
people's reactions to what we will say about Jesus. We fear
being judged by others as being old-fashioned or narrow-
minded and intolerant, or as needing a crutch.

Why would discussing Jesus Christ provoke such reactions? Because the good news of Jesus Christ, though it's the
best news you'll ever hear, is also offensive news. Not only
does the gospel say that Jesus saves, that he makes all things
new, that he forgives and cleanses and makes broken people
whole; the gospel also says that only Jesus saves, that only he
can make all things new, that only he can finally forgive and
cleanse and make us whole.

These words ruffle feathers in our pluralistic society.
"What do you mean, *only* Jesus? How can you, a mere human
in one little corner of the globe, say there is no other name by

which we must be saved? What about *Krishna, Buddha, Mohammed* or *Marx*? What about the salvation promised by Eckankar, est or Scientology?"

As long as we Christians say that Jesus is one of many saviors, we are warmly welcomed at the religious smorgasbord. We are welcomed even if we say that Jesus is the greatest of all the candidates for savior. But once we muster up the courage to say that Jesus is the only savior the world has, we are asked to leave the table.

Who's on Trial?

During Peter and John's trial in Acts, Peter said, "Salvation is found in no one else" (4:12). They also said that the lame man they had prayed for had been healed by Jesus, whom these same accusers had crucified. Notice how the roles in that trial changed. Peter and John were no longer on trial. Jesus was on trial. How ironic! The Jewish leaders who were interrogating Peter and John were the same ones who interrogated Jesus the night before he was executed. They were being given a chance to reverse their previous verdict. But once again they decided to send Jesus away. Once again they came to the verdict that Jesus was not who he claimed to be. And they ordered Peter and John never again to speak in Jesus' name.

Read Acts to see what effect that order had! It was like ordering the earth to stop spinning. Peter and John had found life and salvation in Jesus; and they knew that that life, that salvation, was available to any and all who came to Jesus; and they knew that that life, that salvation, was found *only* in Jesus. They had to keep on speaking in the name of Jesus regardless of the consequences.

"Salvation is found in no one else" is the message the risen Christ asks us to bring to our campuses. And we simply have to accept the fact that this message, this gospel, offends any group that doesn't like absolutes. We have to accept the scandal of particularity—the biblical claim that God has fully revealed himself in one particular person, Jesus of Nazareth, and that God has decisively acted to save the world in this man and only in him.

The world rightly asks, "Why? Why is there no other name by which we can be saved?"

Before answering that question, let's be clear about what we are *not* claiming when we say "there is no other name."

All Truth Is God's

First of all, when we say there is no other name, we are not saying there is no truth in other names. Every culture and religion has some expression of God's truth. Part of the evangelistic task of the church is to search out those truths and show how the gospel of Jesus Christ relates to them. To claim there is no other name but Jesus does not mean other religions and philosophies do not speak any truth. It is, however, to claim that those truths are to be reassessed in the light of Jesus Christ who claims to be the Truth (Jn 14:6).

Second, when we say there is no other name, we are not saying that we can't learn from other names. Christians can learn a great deal from the rest of the world. The intensity with which a Hindu seeks God can make us look like hypocrites. The discipline of a Muslim can make us look very lazy. The total commitment of a Marxist can put us to shame. We have much to learn from people of other faiths and philosophies.

Third, when we say there is no other name, we are not saying that Christianity is the one true religion. Peter was not making any claims for Christianity, for a religion. He was making a claim about a person, Jesus Christ of Nazareth (Acts 4:10). Christianity is not the savior; Christ is. Much of what is called Christianity has not even begun to grasp who Jesus really is. Much of what is called Christianity has not even begun to realize the world-transforming consequences of Jesus' crucifixion and resurrection and subsequent exaltation as Lord. We are not claiming that Christianity is the one and only valid religion. We are claiming that Jesus Christ is the one and only Savior and Lord of the universe. He is the issue, the scandal of particularity.

We come back to the question: Why is there "no other name"? Why is salvation found in no one else? What do we say if a Hindu or Buddhist or Marxist asks us that question?

There are two basic answers to that question: There is no other name (1) because no one else said the things Jesus said; and (2) because no one else did the things that Jesus did.

Jesus' Words

No one else said the things Jesus of Nazareth said. For instance, no one has ever spoken with the authority with which he spoke. That is what struck his listeners after the Sermon on the Mount (Mt 7:28). Other teachers and prophets spoke *by* authority; Jesus spoke *with* authority.

Others introduced their prophecies with the solemn phrase, "Thus saith the Lord." Jesus said, "Truly, truly I say to you." Jesus even set his words in opposition to and over against the words of the religious authorities who came before him. Six times in the Sermon on the Mount he said, "You have heard that it was said . . . but I tell you. . . . " Who is this man who speaks with his own authority?

Also, no one else made himself the issue of his teaching the way Jesus did. He said, "Follow me," while others said follow the law, follow the way of love or follow the Eightfold Path to Enlightenment. Jesus said, "Follow me." Mohammed never made himself the issue of Islam. Buddha never made himself the issue of Buddhism. In fact, Buddha told his disciples that he could do nothing for them—they had to find their own way of enlightenment. A Jewish rabbi once observed that "no Moslem ever sings, 'Mohammed, lover of my soul,' nor does any Jew say of Moses, the Teacher, 'I need thee every hour.' Jesus made himself the issue of his teachings—"Follow *me*," "Abide in me."

Furthermore, no one else made the kind of claims about himself that Jesus did: "I am the bread of life"; "I am the light of the world"; "I am the way and the truth and the life" (Jn 6:35; 8:12; 14:6). No one else, except Yahweh the God of the Hebrews, spoke like this.

Who is this man? Jesus did not simply claim to be a way, a truth, a life. He claimed to be the Way, the Truth, the Life. There is the scandal! Other teachers and prophets say, "Here is the path to life. Live in it." Jesus says, "I am the path. Live in me."

But Jesus said even more. Other teachers and prophets claimed to be sent by God; Jesus claimed to be sent from God. Other teachers claimed to represent God; Jesus claimed that in him God was actually present. He is God in human form. That claim was what generated the hostility of the leaders of Judaism. That claim got him crucified. In *God in the Dock* (Eerdmans), C. S. Lewis said it best: "If you had gone to Buddha and asked him 'Are you the son of Bramah?' he would have said, 'My son, you are still in the vale of illusion.' If you had gone to Socrates and asked, 'Are you Zeus?' he would have laughed at you. If you had gone to Mohammed and asked, 'Are you Allah?' he would first have rent his clothes and then cut your head off. If you had asked Confucius, 'Are you Heaven?,' I think he would have probably replied, 'Remarks which are not in accordance with nature are in bad taste.' "

When the Jews asked Jesus, "Who are you?" he answered, "Just what I have been claiming all along . . . before Abraham was born, I am" (Jn 8:25, 58). There is no other name because no one else said the things that Jesus said.

Jesus' Deeds
But there is a second reason that "salvation is found in no one else." *No one else did the things that Jesus did.* That is, no one else accomplished the kind of salvation Jesus Christ accomplished. No one else has even remotely claimed to do what Jesus claimed to be doing at the cross and through the empty tomb.

Every religious and philosophical system acknowledges that we human beings are caught in some sort of bondage. Jesus understood that bondage in a way no one else did. He saw us as hostages, held by the powers of sin, the demonic and death. And he saw that, try as we might, we cannot free ourselves. Other would-be saviors think we can free ourselves, and they offer steps to liberation. Jesus realized there are no steps out of the prison. So he came to do for us what we could not do for ourselves.

It was at the cross that he met the powers that keep us in bondage. It was at the cross that he fought the agonizing battle for us. For three days it appeared that death had won, that the darkness of death had finally snuffed out the Light of life. But on Easter morning Jesus broke out of the grave! Death had not won after all. He was alive! That fact makes Jesus different from all other saviors. In this man's life, death did not have the last word.

Death is the greatest enemy of life. The fear of death cripples us more than we realize. One could argue that all fear is ultimately rooted in the fear of death. And only Jesus can free us from that fear, for only Jesus has triumphed over death. Once he frees us from the fear of death, we are free to live. We are freed from the tyranny of grabbing for all the gusto because we know there is more to life than our few short years.

There is no other name in the universe by which we must be saved, because no one else said the things Jesus said and no one else did the things he did.

The scandal of particularity is posed by Jesus' own words and deeds. Once we face the fact that he, not we, caused the scandal, we are freed from our fears. Jesus Christ does not call us *to defend* him and his claims and deeds. He calls us to *proclaim* him and his claims and deeds. He can hold his own.

Questions

1. Why is it so difficult to witness for Jesus?
2. What does Johnson mean by "the scandal of particularity"?
3. According to Johnson, what are Christians *not* claiming when they say "There is no other name"? Do you agree with each of Johnson's three statements? Why or why not?
4. How does Jesus differ from other prophets and teachers in what he said about himself? How does he differ in what he did while on earth?

Isn't One Religion as Good as Another?

J.I. Packer

J. I. Packer is a popular conference speaker, author, and theologian. Packer points out that to claim one religion is as good as another assumes that "all worship the same God," but then he proceeds to show the flaw of that argument. He describes the unique features of Christianity as the "three Rs" of the gospel: ruin, redemption, and regeneration.

"All Chinese look alike." This complaint tells you at once two things about the speaker: first, that he is not himself Chinese (a safe bet!), and second, that he lacks interest in Chinese people generally, so that he never looks at any of them very hard. Similarly, if someone asks whether the world's religions are not for all practical purposes the same, it suggests first that he knows and cares little about religions in general, and second that he is not committed to any one religion in particular—for if he was, he would be sure that the answer to his question is *no!*

Commitment and judgment

But would a committed man be the right person to judge? Is not an uncommitted attitude a help to clearer discernment? No—not at the deepest level, anyway. So far from the uncommitted man being able to discern the truth about all religions, he cannot fully appreciate any of them. The onlooker is supposed to see most of the game, but in matters where commitment is involved mere detached observers make poor judges. It is those who have taken the plunge, not those who gather goose-pimples on the edge, who really know what the water is like. Bachelors cannot in the nature of the case be profound authorities on married life, nor the non-religious on religions.

The chances are that the question under discussion would only ever be asked by someone recoiling, in conscious non-acceptance, from the claims of one particular faith. Certainly, all the world's great religions do in fact claim to be true, final, and exclusive, and one of the marks of their adherents is that they make these claims their own, and show the courage of their convictions by judging that those who reject these claims are, to that extent, wrong. No Jew, Christian, Moslem, or Buddhist could countenance the suggestion that one religion is as good as another. This must be stressed at the outset.

Good for what?

The more one thinks about the suggestion, the odder it seems. "Good for what?" one asks. The great religions do not claim to be good for the same thing! Christianity points the road to endless fellowship with God; Buddhism and Hinduism profess only to plot the path to final personal extinction. Nor can it be blithely assumed, as is so often done, that we all worship the same God. Tribal religions are polytheistic, each with a different quota of deities; Hinduism is pantheistic; Buddhism is atheistic; and among monotheistic faiths, Judaism and Islam are as strongly unitarian as Christianity is Trinitarian!

A century ago, when comparative religion as a science was in its infancy, some German thinkers embraced the idea that there is a "highest common factor" of religions, a sense of kinship with God which is common property, but which different religions express with varying degrees of adequacy. On this view, Christianity is certainly the Rolls-Royce among religions, the best of its kind, but the same sense of oneness with God underlies them all, just as the same basic design is found in all cars. Hence Kipling's sentiment: "Many roads thou hast fashioned; all of them lead to the light." Or, as one often hears it put: "We're all climbing the same mountain; we shall meet at the top." Here, too, the sustained quest, in certain university exam papers, for "the definition of religion," as if the heart of religion everywhere was the same. However, closer study of non-Christian faiths in this century has shown that the likenesses between them and Christianity are on the surface only; in basic outlook they are poles apart from the faith which acknowledges Jesus of Nazareth as divine Saviour and Lord, and as such, God's last word to man.

Some might answer the question "Good for what?" by saying "Good for meeting certain universally felt needs"—such as the need for inner tranquillity and detachment. This is to reduce all religion to do-it-yourself psychiatry, or yoga—psycho-physical self-culture. The claim made by all religions, however, is to bring a true message about the universe and the powers behind it, and to show the way of adjustment, not merely to yourself, but to your whole cosmic environment. And the fact we must face is that the messages are at variance, so that you have to choose between them. Not more than one of them can be true.

The uniqueness of Christianity

This is the place to stress the uniqueness of Christianity, which differs more radically from other world-religions than any of them differ from each other. Old preachers spoke of the "three Rs" of the gospel: *Ruin, Redemption,* and *Regeneration.* Under these headings the most distinctive features of Christianity fall.

Ruin. Other faiths assume our ability to secure and retain God's favour by right action, and give us detailed guidance as to how to do it; but Christianity says that sin has so ruined us that we cannot do this. It is beyond our power to keep the law of God as we should; we are guilty and helpless, wholly unable to save ourselves, and so must be saved, if at all, by the action of another (Romans 8:8, 9:30-10:13; Galatians 2:21, 3:10-12; Ephesians 2:1-9; Titus 3:3-7).

Redemption. Other faiths direct us to follow the teaching of their founders, famous men long deceased; but Christianity, identifying its founder as God incarnate, who died for our sins and rose again to bestow forgiveness, proclaims him as alive and calls on us to trust him and his atoning work, making him the object of our worship and service henceforth. Despite various pagan myths (which C. S. Lewis called "good dreams") about saviours of one kind or another, redemption through the love of the son of God, who became man, bore his father's judgment on our sins, and rose from death to reign for ever, is a theme without parallel in the world's religions (Romans 3:23-26, 4:24 f., 5:6-10; Galatians 2:20, 3:13 f.; 2 Corinthians 5:18-21; 1 John 4:8-10; Revelation 5; Acts 16:30 f.)

Regeneration. Christianity proclaims that those who repent of sin and trust in Jesus Christ are created anew at the heart of their being by the Holy Spirit. They are united to Jesus Christ in his risen life; their inner nature is changed, so that their deepest impulse is not now to disobey God and serve self, but to deny self and obey God. Thus they are born again into a new life of fellowship with Christ, assurance of forgiveness and sonship to God, and unconquerable hope and joy. There is nothing like this in any other religion (John 3:3-15; Romans 6:1-14, 8:16-39; 2 Corinthians 5:14-17; Colossians 2:10-15, 3:1-4; 1 Peter 1:3-13).

The Christian picture of other religions

A final unique feature of Christianity is that, though other religions do not explain it, it explains them. In Romans 1:18-25 Paul accounts for the prevalence of idolatry in terms of sinful man the world over suppressing and distorting the "general revelation" of God and his claims as Creator which is given to us in and with our knowledge of created things. Paul sees man as having an inescapable sense of God which obliges him to worship something, yet as having an antipathy to God, induced by sin, which impels him not to worship the God who made him. So he distorts and falsifies the knowledge of God given him in general revelation. Hence spring the many forms of non-Christian religion, all containing details that are right in an overall setting that is wrong, and all conspicuously lacking knowledge of God's forgiveness in Christ, of which general revelation tells nothing.

Scripture does not regard non-Christian religion as saving. Jesus Christ must be proclaimed to all the world, and men everywhere must be called to turn "to God from idols, to serve a living and true God" through Jesus' mediation (1 Thessalonians 1:9 RSV), for "there is no other name under heaven given among men by which we must be saved" (Acts 4:12).

Questions

1. Why do nonreligious people make poor judges of religion?
2. What are the distinctive features of Christianity? How do they set Christianity apart from other religions?
3. What important feature of Christianity does general revelation fail to reveal? How is this feature made known to humankind?
4. Suppose a friend walked up to you one day and said, "Isn't one religion as good as another?" How would you reply? (Weave the "three Rs" of the gospel into your answer.)

1.) Non-Religious people make poor judges of religion because they have not Known a religion nor are they committing to one. No point of contact.

2.) Distinct features.
  Ruin — Man is a sinner & cannot save himself. Only God through the redemptive work of Jesus can save man.

  Redemption — Christianity identifies the work of Jesus on the cross as the one act which redeems man to God.

  Regeneration — Once saved man has a new life with God forever.

3.) God's forgiveness in Christ. It must be proclaimed by men.

4.) a) Each religion is distinct
    b) Christianity is unique ......

How Can I Believe in a God Who Allows Evil and Suffering?

The Deer at Providencia

Annie Dillard

Annie Dillard is a Pulitzer Prize-winning writer and teach-er of fiction. This selection is excerpted from her book Teach-ing a Stone to Talk. *Dillard describes two scenes of suffer-ing. One is a deer roped to a tree in an Ecuadorian village she is visiting. The deer's neck is rubbed raw and its feet become tangled as it struggles in vain for freedom. Dillard also has a clipping taped to her mirror of a man who has been severely burned twice in 13 years. Would someone explain "what is going on" to that deer and to the man, Dillard asks. "And send me the carbon."*

There were four of us North Americans in the jungle, in the Ecuadorian jungle on the banks of the Napo River in the Amazon watershed. The other three North Americans were metropolitan men. We stayed in tents in one riverside village, and visited others. At the village called Providencia we saw a sight which moved us, and which shocked the men.

The first thing we saw when we climbed the riverbank to the village of Providencia was the deer. It was roped to a tree on the grass clearing near the thatch shelter where we would eat lunch.

The deer was small, about the size of a whitetail fawn, but apparently full-grown. It had a rope around its neck and three feet caught in the rope. Someone said that the dogs had caught it that morning and the villagers were going to cook and eat it that night.

This clearing lay at the edge of the little thatched-hut village. We could see the villagers going about their business, scattering feed corn for hens about their houses, and wandering down paths to the river to bathe. The village headman was our host; he stood beside us as we watched the deer struggle. Several village boys were interested in the deer; they formed part of the circle we made around it in the clearing. So also did four businessmen from Quito who were attempting to guide us around the jungle. Few of the very different people standing in this circle had a common language. We watched the deer, and no one said much.

The deer lay on its side at the rope's very end, so the rope lacked slack to let it rest its head in the dust. It was "pretty," delicate of bone like all deer, and thin-skinned for the tropics. Its skin looked virtually hairless, in fact, and almost translucent, like a membrane. Its neck was no thicker than my wrist; it was rubbed open on the rope, and gashed. Trying to paw itself free of the rope, the deer had scratched its own neck with its hooves. The raw underside of its neck showed red stripes and some bruises bleeding inside the muscles. Now three of its feet were hooked in the rope under its jaw. It could not stand, of course, on one leg, so it could not move to slacken the rope and ease the pull on its throat and enable it to rest its head.

Repeatedly the deer paused, motionless, its eyes veiled, with only its rib cage in motion, and its breaths the only sound. Then, after I would think, "It has given up; now it will die," it would heave. The rope twanged; the tree leaves clattered; the deer's free foot beat the ground. We stepped back and held our breaths. It thrashed, kicking, but only one leg moved; the other three legs tightened inside the rope's loop. Its hip jerked; its spine shook. Its eyes rolled; its tongue, thick with spittle, pushed in and out. Then it would rest again. We watched this for fifteen minutes.

Once three young native boys charged in, released its trapped legs, and jumped back to the circle of people. But instantly the deer scratched up its neck with its hooves and snared its forelegs in the rope again. It was easy to imagine a third and then a fourth leg soon stuck, like Brer Rabbit and the Tar Baby.

We watched the deer from the circle, and then we drifted on to lunch. Our palm-roofed shelter stood on a grassy promontory from which we could see the deer tied to the tree, pigs and hens walking under village houses, and black-and-white cattle standing in the river. There was even a breeze.

Lunch, which was the second and better lunch we had that day, was hot and fried. There was a big fish called *doncella*, a kind of catfish, dipped whole in corn flour and beaten egg, then deep fried. With our fingers we pulled soft fragments of it from its sides to our plates, and ate; it was delicate fish-flesh, fresh and mild. Someone found the roe, and I ate of that too—it was fat and stronger, like egg yolk, naturally enough, and warm.

There was also a stew of meat in shreds with rice and pale brown gravy. I had asked what kind of deer it was tied to the tree; Pepe had answered in Spanish, *"Gama."* Now they told us this was *gama* too, stewed. I suspect the word means merely game or venison. At any rate, I heard that the village dogs had cornered another deer just yesterday, and it was this deer which we were now eating in full sight of the whole article. It was good. I was surprised at its tenderness. But it is a fact that high levels of lactic acid, which builds up in muscle tissues during exertion, tenderizes.

After the fish and meat we ate bananas fried in chunks and

served on a tray; they were sweet and full of flavor. I felt terrific. My shirt was wet and cool from swimming; I had had a night's sleep, two decent walks, three meals, and a swim— everything tasted good. From time to time each one of us, separately, would look beyond our shaded roof to the sunny spot where the deer was still convulsing in the dust. Our meal completed, we walked around the deer and back to the boats.

That night I learned that while we were watching the deer, the others were watching me.

We four North Americans grew close in the jungle in a way that was not the usual artificial intimacy of travelers. We liked each other. We stayed up all that night talking, murmuring, as though we rocked on hammocks slung above time. The others were from big cities: New York, Washington, Boston. They all said that I had no expression on my face when I was watching the deer—or at any rate, not the expression they expected.

They had looked to see how I, the only woman, and the youngest, was taking the sight of the deer's struggles. I looked detached, apparently, or hard, or calm, or focused, still. I don't know. I was thinking. I remember feeling very old and energetic. I could say like Thoreau that I have traveled widely in Roanoke, Virginia. I have thought a great deal about carnivorousness; I eat meat. These things are not issues; they are mysteries.

Gentlemen of the city, what surprises you? That there is suffering here, or that I know it?

We lay in the tent and talked. "If it had been my wife," one man said with special vigor, amazed, "she wouldn't have cared *what* was going on; she would have dropped *everything* right at that moment and gone in the village from here to there to there, she would not have *stopped* until that animal was out of its suffering one way or another. She couldn't *bear* to see a creature in agony like that."

I nodded.

Now I am home. When I wake I comb my hair before the mirror above my dresser. Every morning for the past two years I have seen in that mirror, beside my sleep-softened face, the blackened face of a burnt man. It is a wire-service photograph clipped from a newspaper and taped to my mirror. The caption reads: "Alan McDonald in Miami hospital bed." All you can see in the photograph is a smudged triangle of face from his eyelids to his lower lip; the rest is bandages. You cannot see the expression in his eyes; the bandages shade them.

The story, headed MAN BURNED FOR SECOND TIME, begins:

"Why does God hate me?" Alan McDonald asked from his hospital bed.

"When the gunpowder went off, I couldn't believe it," he said. "I just couldn't believe it. I said, 'No, God couldn't do this to me again.'"

He was in a burn ward in Miami, in serious condition. I do not even know if he lived. I wrote him a letter at the time, cringing.

He had been burned before, thirteen years previously, by flaming gasoline. For years he had been having his body restored and his face remade in dozens of operations. He had been a boy, and then a burnt boy. He had already been stunned by what could happen, by how life could veer.

Once I read that people who survive bad burns tend to go crazy; they have a very high suicide rate. Medicine cannot ease their pain; drugs just leak away, soaking the sheets, because there is no skin to hold them in. The people just lie there and weep. Later they kill themselves. They had not known, before they were burned, that the world included such suffering, that life could permit them personally such pain.

This time a bowl of gunpowder had exploded on McDonald.

"I didn't realize what had happened at first," he recounted. "And then I heard that sound from 13 years ago. I was burning. I rolled to put the fire out and I thought, 'Oh God, not again.'

"If my friend hadn't been there, I would have jumped into a canal with a rock around my neck."

His wife concludes the piece, "Man, it just isn't fair."

I read the whole clipping again every morning. This is the Big Time here, every minute of it. Will someone please explain to Alan McDonald in his dignity, to the deer at Providencia in his dignity, what is going on? And mail me the carbon.

When we walked by the deer at Providencia for the last time, I said to Pepe, with a pitying glance at the deer, "*Pobrecito* "—"poor little thing." But I was trying out Spanish. I knew at the time it was a ridiculous thing to say.

Questions

1. Why did Dillard show no apparent pity or horror as she watched the deer struggle? Was she uncaring or just "able to handle it"?
2. Why do you think Dillard has the McDonald clipping taped to her mirror? Do you think that it is a bit strange to read it through every day? Why do you think she does so?
3. What basic questions is Dillard trying to find answers for?
4. Why do you think God allows suffering?

Aprille

Garrison Keillor

Garrison Keillor is a master storyteller and humorist who is well known for his live radio programs and frequent magazine articles. He is the creator of the little Minnesota town of Lake Wobegon where Lois Tollerud and her family live. In this selection, Lois has a crisis of faith just hours before she is to be confirmed in Lake Wobegon Lutheran Church. She discovers that when she prays, she hears "something like an echo," as if the prayer is "only in her head."

It has been a quiet week in Lake Wobegon. Spring has come, grass is green, the trees are leafing out, birds arriving every day by the busload, and now the Norwegian bachelor farmers are washing their sheets. In town the windows are open, so, as you pause in your walk to admire Mrs. Hoglund's rock garden, you can smell her floor wax and hear the piano lesson she is giving, the tune that goes "da da Da da Da da da," and up by school, smell the macaroni cheese hot dish for lunch and hear from upstairs the voices of Miss Melrose's class reciting Chaucer.

> Whan that Aprille with his shoures soote
> The droghte of March hath perced to the roote
> And bathed every veyne in swich licour
> Of which vertu engendred is the flour;
> Whan Zephyrus eek with his sweete breeth
> Inspired hath in every holt and heeth
> The tendre croppes, and the yonge sonne
> Hath in the Ram his halve cours yronne
> And smale fowles maken melodye
> That slepen al the nyght with open ye . . .

The words are six hundred years old and describe spring in this little town quite well; the sweet breath of the wind, the youth of the sun, the sweet rain, the tendre croppes, the smale fowles maken melodye: we have them all.

I made a pilgrimage up there last Sunday to visit my family and my family wasn't there. I walked in, called; there was no answer.

I drove over to Aunt Flo's to look for them and got caught in Sunday-morning rush hour. It was Confirmation Sunday at Lake Wobegon Lutheran Church. Thirteen young people had their faith confirmed and were admitted to the circle of believers, thirteen dressed-up boys and girls at the altar rail in front of a crowd of every available relative. Pastor Ingqvist asked them all the deepest questions about the faith (questions that have troubled theologians for years), which these young people answered readily from memory and then partook of their first communion. Later they lounged around on the front steps and asked each other, "Were you scared?" and said, "No, I really wasn't, not as much as I thought I'd be," and went home to eat chuck roast, and some of them had their first real cup of coffee. They found it to be a bitter oily drink that makes you dizzy and sick to your stomach, but they were Lutherans now and that's what Lutherans drink.

The Tolleruds, for example, drank gallons of coffee on Sunday. Church had been two hours long, the regular service plus confirmation, and Lutherans don't have the opportunity to stand up and kneel down and get exercise that you find elsewhere, so everyone was stiff and dopey, and the Tolleruds, when they sit around and visit, are all so quiet and agreeable they get drowsy, so they drink plenty of coffee. Years ago, when Uncle Gunnar was alive, they didn't need so much. He had wild white hair and eyebrows the size of mice, he spilled food down himself and didn't care, he had whiskey on his breath, and if anyone mentioned the Lutheran church he said, "*Haw!*" He was an old bachelor who got rich from founding a chain of private clubs in the Dakotas and Iowa called the Quality Prestige Clubs. They were only empty rooms over a drugstore with some old leather couches and a set of *Collier's Encyclopedia*, and he gave away memberships to men who'd never been invited to join a club before, tall sad men with thin dry hair, of whom there are a lot, and made his money selling them lots of shirts and ties and cufflinks with the QP insignia. Uncle Gunnar got rich and sold the Clubs to an Iowa meat packer and went to Australia to get into some line of work down there he didn't consider worth mentioning, and the last anyone saw him was in 1962. Presumably he died, unless perhaps he just got tired of us knowing him.

The Tolleruds gathered for pot roast because Daryl and Marilyn's daughter Lois was confirmed. She sat at the head of the table, next to her dad, promoted from the children's table out in the kitchen. She is a tall lanky girl who has grown four inches this year, and it has tired her out. She is quieter than she used to be, a tall shy girl with long brown hair she has learned to tie in an elegant bun, and creamy skin that she keeps beautiful by frequent blushing, which is good for the circulation and makes her lovelier whenever she is admired.

A boy who has sat silently across from her in geometry since September has written her a twenty-seven-page letter in small print telling her how he feels about her (since September he's looked as if he was just about to talk, and now it all comes out at once: he thinks God has written their names together in the Book of Love). But she wasn't thinking about him Sunday—she was blushing to see her Confirmation cake with the Scripture verse inscribed in blue frosting: "Be not conformed to this world: but be ye transformed by the renewing of your mind, that ye may prove what is that good, and acceptable, and perfect, will of God." It was a large cake, and Marilyn used the extra-fine nozzle on the frosting gun—there it sat, lit with birthday candles, and Lois didn't know how to tell them that she wasn't sure that she believed in God. She was pretty sure that she might've lost her faith.

She thought she might've lost it on Friday night or sometime Saturday morning, she wasn't sure. She didn't mention it at that time because she thought she might get it back.

On Friday night, less than forty-eight hours before confirmation, she was sitting on the couch watching television with Dave, the boy who wrote the letter, while her mom and dad were gone to have supper with her prayer parents. When you're confirmed, you're assigned prayer parents, a couple who promise to pray for you for three months prior, and Lois's turned out to be the Val Tollefsons, people she had never liked. To think that every night over supper Val Tollefson had bowed his big thick head and said, "And, Lord, we ask Thee to strengthen Lois in her faith"—the same man who said once, "You won't amount to a hill of beans, you don't have the sense that God gave geese." She could feel her faith slip a little. She felt guilty, because Dave wasn't supposed to be there, and she was supposed to be ironing her confirmation dress, but he had walked two miles from his house, so what could she do? She felt sorry for Dave, he always has a bad haircut and a swarm of pimples on his forehead, but she likes him, he's quiet and nice. They talked to each other at Luther League get-togethers about what it would be like to be someone else, someone famous, for example, like Willie Nelson—you could use your fame to do good—and they went for one walk halfway around the lake, holding hands, and then she got the long letter saying how much she meant to him, twenty-seven pages, which was much more than she wanted to mean to him; it scared her.

She didn't know that Dave was a born writer, that twenty-seven pages is nothing to him, he did thirty-one on the death of his dog, Buff—she told him it would be better if they didn't see each other anymore. Friday night he walked over, full of more to say. She had four little brothers and a sister to take care of, so he sat on the old red sofa with a bottle of orange pop and watched as she fed the baby, and she turned on the TV and lost her faith. Men in khaki suits were beating people senseless, shooting them with machine guns, throwing the bodies out of helicopters. Their reception was so poor, the picture so fuzzy, it was more like radio, which made the horrors worse, and she thought, "This could happen here." It gave her a cold chill to imagine violent strange men busting in, as they had done to Anne Frank. She held the baby, Karen, imagining all of them were hiding from Nazis, and heard twigs crunch outside and knew that this boy could not protect her. She prayed and heard something like an echo, as if the prayer was only in her head. The whole world in the control of dark powers, working senseless evil in our lives, and prayer went no place, prayer just went up the chimney like smoke.

When Marilyn cut the confirmation cake and served it with butter-brickle ice cream, Lois thought, "I should say something." Like "I don't believe in God, I don't think." Nobody would need coffee then.

After dinner she put on her jeans and a white jacket and walked out across the cornfield toward the road and the ravine to think about her faith on this cloudy day, and, walking west over a little rise, she saw, just beyond the ravine, a white car she'd never seen before, and a strange man in a trenchcoat standing beside it. She walked toward him, thinking of the parable of the Good Samaritan, thinking that perhaps God was calling her to go witness to him and thereby recover her faith. He stood and pitched stones up over the trees, and as she got closer, he turned and smiled, put out his hand, and came toward her. She saw her mistake. Something glittered in his mouth. She stopped. He was a killer come looking for someone, it didn't matter to him who it was, anyone who came down the road would do. He walked toward her; she turned and fell down and said, "Oh please no, please God no."

I hadn't seen her for five years. I said, "Lois, Lois—it's me." I helped her up. How are you? It's good to see you again. We shuffled along the rim of the ravine, looking for the thin path down, and she told me about her confirmation, which I have an interest in because I am her godfather. I wasn't invited to church, I reckon, because fourteen years ago I wasn't anyone's first choice for godfather. I was nominated by Marilyn because Daryl suggested his brother Gunnar and she thought that was ridiculous, and to show Daryl what a poor choice he would be she suggested me, and Daryl said, "Sure, fine, if that's what you want," and they were stuck with me.

The baby was named for her mother's Sunday-school teacher, who was my aunt Lois, my youngest aunt, so young she was like an older sister. She was single when I was a boy and so had plenty of time for her favorite nephew. She told me I was. She said, Don't tell the others but you are the one I love more than anyone else, or words to that effect. We were riding the bus to Minneapolis, she and I, to visit Great-aunt Posie. Lois seemed young to me because she loved to pretend. We imagined the bus was our private bus and we could go anywhere we wanted. We were *somebody*.

My favorite game was Strangers, pretending we didn't know each other. I'd get up and walk to the back of the bus and turn around and come back to the seat and say, "Do you mind if I sit here?" And she said, "No, I don't mind," and I'd sit. And she'd say: "A very pleasant day, isn't it?"

We didn't speak this way in our family, but she and I were strangers, and so we could talk as we pleased.

"Are you going all the way to Minneapolis, then?"

"As a matter of fact, ma'am, I'm going to New York City. I'm in a very successful hit play on Broadway, and I came back out here to Minnesota because my sweet old aunt died, and I'm going back to Broadway now on the evening plane. Then next week I go to Paris, France, where I currently reside on the Champs-Elysées. My name is Tom Flambeau, perhaps you've read about me."

"No, I never heard of you in my life, but I'm very sorry to hear about your aunt. She must have been a wonderful person."

"Oh, she was pretty old. She was all right, I guess."

"Are you very close to your family, then?"

"No, not really. I'm adopted, you see. My real parents were Broadway actors—they sent me out to the farm thinking I'd get more to eat, but I don't think that people out here understand people like me."

She looked away from me. She looked out the window a long time. I'd hurt her feelings. Minutes passed. But I didn't know her. Then I said, "Talk to me. Please."

She said, "Sir, if you bother me anymore I'll have the driver throw you off this bus."

"Say that you know me. Please."

And when I couldn't bear it one more second, she touched me and I was myself again.

And the next time we rode the bus, I said, "Let's pretend we don't know each other."

She said, "No, you get too scared."

"I won't this time." I got up and came back and said, "It's a very pleasant day, isn't it? Are you going to Minneapolis?"

Eventually we do. We pretend to be someone else and need them to say they know us, but one day we become that person and they simply don't know us. From that there is no bus back that I know of.

Lois Tollerud asked me, "Why did you stop here?" I told her I had parked by the ravine, looking for a spot where our Boy Scout troop used to camp and where Einar Tingvold the scoutmaster got so mad at us once, he threw two dozen eggs one by one into the woods. Each egg made him madder and he threw it farther. When he ran out of eggs he reached for something else. It was his binoculars. He didn't want to throw them away but he was so furious he couldn't stop—he threw the binoculars and reached for them in the same motion. Heaved them and tried to grab the strap as it went by. We scouts looked for it for a whole afternoon, thirty years ago. Whenever I go by the ravine, I look for a reflection of glass, thinking that, if I found those binoculars by some wonderful luck and took them back to him, he might forgive me.

"That's not true, is it?" she said. "No, it's not."

I stopped there because, frankly, I'd had a lot of coffee, but I couldn't tell her that. We walked for almost a mile along that ravine, to the lake and back, and then I felt like I'd like to visit her family after all.

We walked in. I got a fairly warm hello, and was offered coffee. "In a minute," I said. "Excuse me, I'll be right back." I had a cup and a slice of cake that said "Con but for," a little triangle out of her verse.

Be not conformed to this world: but be ye transformed. Our lovely world has the power to make us brave. A person wants to be someone else and gets scared and needs to be known, but we ride so far on that bus, we become the stranger. Nevertheless these things stay the same: the sweet breath, the rain, the tendre croppes, and the smale fowles maken melodye—God watches each one and knows when it falls, and so much more does He watch us all.

Questions

1. Why does Lois doubt her faith? How has she become a stranger to her own family?
2. How is she like the "tall sad men" whom Uncle Gunnar signs up for the Quality Prestige Club? What motivates them to join?
3. What words would you use to describe her suffering? Is her suffering more than a spiritual crisis?

Night

Elie Wiesel

Elie Wiesel is a writer and college professor whose many books and articles have dealt largely with the Holocaust. This selection is excerpted from his book Night, *in which he describes the horror he felt and saw as he and his family arrived at the Nazi death camp Auschwitz. Although raised in a God-fearing Jewish home, Wiesel says that it was his initial moments at Auschwitz that "murdered my God and my soul and turned my dreams to dust."*

The cherished objects we had brought with us thus far were left behind in the train, and with them, at last, our illusions.

Every two yards or so an SS man held his tommy gun trained on us. Hand in hand we followed the crowd.

An SS noncommissioned officer came to meet us, a truncheon in his hand. He gave the order:

"Men to the left! Women to the right!"

Eight words spoken quietly, indifferently, without emotion. Eight short, simple words. Yet that was the moment when I parted from my mother. I had not had time to think, but already I felt the pressure of my father's hand: we were alone. For a part of a second I glimpsed my mother and my sisters moving way to the right. Tzipora held Mother's hand. I saw them disappear into the distance; my mother was stroking my sister's fair hair, as though to protect her, while I walked on with my father and the other men. And I did not know that in that place, at that moment, I was parting from my mother and Tzipora forever. I went on walking. My father held onto my hand.

Behind me, an old man fell to the ground. Near him was

an SS man, putting his revolver back in its holster.

My hand shifted on my father's arm. I had one thought—not to lose him. Not to be left alone.

The SS officers gave the order:

"Form fives!"

Commotion. At all costs we must keep together.

"Here, kid, how old are you?"

It was one of the prisoners who asked me this. I could not see his face, but his voice was tense and weary.

"I'm not quite fifteen yet."

"No. Eighteen."

"But I'm not," I said. "Fifteen."

"Fool. Listen to what *I* say."

Then he questioned my father, who replied:

"Fifty."

The other grew more furious than ever.

"No, not fifty. Forty. Do you understand? Eighteen and forty."

He disappeared into the night shadows. A second man came up, spitting oaths at us.

"What have you come here for, you sons of bitches? What are you doing here, eh?"

Someone dared to answer him.

"What do you think? Do you suppose we've come here for our own pleasure? Do you think we asked to come?"

A little more, and the man would have killed him.

"You shut your trap, you filthy swine, or I'll squash you right now! You'd have done better to have hanged yourselves where you were than to come here. Didn't you know what was in store for you at Auschwitz? Haven't you heard about it? In 1944?"

No, we had not heard. No one had told us. He could not believe his ears. His tone of voice became increasingly brutal.

"Do you see that chimney over there? See it? Do you see those flames? (Yes, we did see the flames.) Over there—that's where you're going to be taken. That's your grave, over there. Haven't you realized it yet? You dumb bastards, don't you understand anything? You're going to be burned. Frizzled away. Turned into ashes."

He was growing hysterical in his fury. We stayed motionless, petrified. Surely it was all a nightmare? An unimaginable nightmare?

I heard murmurs around me.

"We've got to do something. We can't let ourselves be killed. We can't go like beasts to the slaughter. We've got to revolt."

There were a few sturdy young fellows among us. They had knives on them, and they tried to incite the others to throw themselves on the armed guards.

One of the young men cried:

"Let the world learn of the existence of Auschwitz. Let everybody hear about it, while they can still escape. . . . "

But the older ones begged their children not to do anything foolish:

"You must never lose faith, even when the sword hangs over your head. That's the teaching of our sages. . . . "

The wind of revolt died down. We continued our march toward the square. In the middle stood the notorious Dr. Mengele (a typical SS officer: a cruel face, but not devoid of intelligence, and wearing a monocle); a conductor's baton in his hand, he was standing among the other officers. The baton moved unremittingly, sometimes to the right, sometimes to the left.

I was already in front of him:

"How old are you?" he asked, in an attempt at a paternal tone of voice.

"Eighteen." My voice was shaking.

"Are you in good health?"

"Yes."

"What's your occupation?"

Should I say that I was a student?

"Farmer," I heard myself say.

This conversation cannot have lasted more than a few seconds. It had seemed like an eternity to me.

The baton moved to the left. I took half a step forward. I wanted to see first where they were sending my father. If he went to the right, I would go after him.

The baton once again pointed to the left for him too. A weight was lifted from my heart.

We did not yet know which was the better side, right or left; which road led to prison and which to the crematory. But for the moment I was happy; I was near my father. Our procession continued to move slowly forward.

Another prisoner came up to us:

"Satisfied?"

"Yes," someone replied.

"Poor devils, you're going to the crematory."

He seemed to be telling the truth. Nor far from us, flames were leaping up from a ditch, gigantic flames. They were burning something. A lorry drew up at the pit and delivered its load—little children. Babies! Yes, I saw it—saw it with my own eyes . . . those children in the flames. (Is it surprising that I could not sleep after that? Sleep had fled from my eyes.)

So this was where we were going. A little farther on was another and larger ditch for adults.

I pinched my face. Was I still alive? Was I awake? I could not believe it. How could it be possible for them to burn people, children and for the world to keep silent? No, none of this could be true. It was a nightmare. . . . Soon I should wake with a start, my heart pounding, and find myself back in the bedroom of my childhood, among y books. . . .

My father's voice drew me from my thoughts:

"It's a shame . . . a shame that you couldn't have gone with your mother. . . . I saw several boys of your age going with their mothers. . . ."

His voice was terribly sad. I realized that he did not want to see what they were going to do to me. He did not want to see the burning of his only son.

My forehead was bathed in cold sweat. But I told him that I did not believe that they could burn people in our age, that humanity would never tolerate it. . . .

"Humanity? Humanity is not concerned with us. Today anything is allowed. Anything is possible, even these cremato- ries . . . "

His voice was choking.

"Father," I said, "if that is so, I don't want to wait here. I'm going to run to the electric wire. That would be better than slow agony in the flames."

He did not answer. He was weeping. His body was shaken convulsively. Around us, everyone was weeping. Someone began to recite the Kaddish, the prayer for the dead. I do not know it it has ever happened before, in the long history of the Jews, that people have ever recited the prayer for the dead for themselves.

"*Yitgadal veyitkadach shmé raba.* . . . May His Name be blessed and magnified. . . . " whispered my father.

For the first time, I felt revolt rise up in me. Why should I bless His name? The Eternal, Lord of the Universe, the All-Powerful and Terrible, was silent. What had I to thank Him for?

We continued our march. We were gradually drawing clos- er to the ditch, from which an infernal heat was rising. Still twenty steps to go. If I wanted to bring about my own death, this was the moment. Our line had now only fifteen paces to cover. I bit my lips so that my father would not hear my teeth chattering. Ten steps still. Eight. Seven. We marched slowly on, as though following a hearse at our own funeral. Four steps more. Three steps. There it was now, right in front of us, the pit and its flames. I gathered all that was left of my strength, so that I could break from the ranks and throw myself on the barbed wire. In the depths of my heart, I bade farewell to my father, to the whole universe; and, in spite of myself, the words formed themselves and issued in a whisper from my lips: *Yit- gadal veyitkadach shmé raba.* . . . May His Name be blessed and magnified. . . . My heart was bursting. The moment had come. I was face to face with the Angel of Death. . . .

No. Two steps from the pit we were ordered to turn to the left and made to go into a barracks.

I pressed my father's hand. He said:

"Do you remember Madame Schächter, in the train?"

Never shall I forget that night the first night in camp, which has turned my life into one long night, seven times cursed and seven times sealed. Never shall I forget that smoke. Never shall I forget the little faces of the children, whose bodies I saw turned into wreaths of smoke beneath a silent blue sky.

Never shall I forget those flames which consumed my faith forever.

Never shall I forget that nocturnal silence which deprived me, for all eternity, of the desire to live. Never shall I forget those moments which murdered my God and my soul and turned my dreams to dust. Never shall I forget these things, even if I am condemned to live as long as God Himself. Never.

Questions

1. What effect did Auschwitz have on Elie Wiesel's faith in God?
2. Do you think God's silence is the same as God's judgment? Why or why not?

The Problem of Evil

Peter Kreeft

Peter Kreeft is a college professor and author who often writes in a style which dramatizes both sides of a moral issue, as he does in this selection. Sal is not a Christian, but is a very open-minded seeker. Chris is a Christian who tries to answer Sal's questions from a biblical framework. Sal's questioning deals primarily with the problem of evil: If God is completely good and completely powerful, how can there be suffering, death, and injustice in the world?

Sal: Chris, I've got a real tough one for you today.

Chris: A tough question?

Sal: Yes.

Chris: I don't have *all* the answers, you know.

Sal: Well, I sure hope you have the answer to this one, because it's the best argument against God I've ever seen.

Chris: Oh, the problem of evil?

Sal: How did you know that was the one I meant?

Chris: It's the *only* really tough argument against God. How would you put it?

Sal: This way. It sounds awfully simple and unanswerable. God is supposed to be completely good, right?

Chris: Right.

Sal: And also completely powerful, right?

Chris: Right.

Sal:. And evil things really happen, right?

Chris: Right. Terrible things. Suffering and death and injustice.

Sal. Well, if there's a God running the world with His power, then He must want these bad things to happen, and then He's not good. And if God doesn't want them to happen and they do anyway, then He's not all-powerful.

Chris: That's a very strong way of putting the argument.

Sal: I don't want a compliment. I want an answer.

Chris: Let's begin by distinguishing two different questions about evil. The first question is where evil came from. Did God make it? The second question is where it's going to end up. What's God doing about it? Why doesn't he destroy it all right now?

Sal: Now you've got *two* questions to answer instead of one. You're making it harder for yourself .

Chris: No, I'm just trying to get rid of confusion so that I can answer the two questions in different ways.

Sal: Well, let's hear your answer to the first one. Didn't God make everything?

Chris: Yes.

Sal: Then He must have made evil too. How can a good God make evil?

Chris: He didn't make evil.

Sal: But you just said He made everything.

Chris: Yes. Evil's not a thing. He made every *thing*.

Sal: You mean evil isn't real?

Chris: Of course it's real. I didn't say that. I said it's not a *thing*.

Sal: What is it, then?

Chris: Look here: if I hit you with a rock, that's evil, right?

Sal: I'll say.

Chris: But the *rock* isn't evil, is it?

Sal: No. In fact you have to find a *good* rock to hit me with.

Chris: Well, is my hand evil?

Sal: No. You have two good hands.

Chris: So what *is* evil? The choice to hit you is evil. The act of hitting you is evil.

Sal: That's right.

Chris: Well, God didn't make that choice or that act. I did.

Sal: I thought God made everything.

Chris: Every *thing*, yes. Every rock and hand and fish and star and atom and angel, yes. But He didn't make my choices or my acts. I make them with my own free will. If I choose evil, I'm to blame, not God.

Sal: But He created you.

Chris: Yes, but He created me good. I'm not evil until I choose to do an evil act.

Sal: But God gave you the power to do evil acts and the power to freely choose evil in your will.

Chris: Yes, but power isn't evil by itself. Only using it in the wrong way is evil. The power in my arm is good. God gave it to me, and He wants me to use it for good. If I use it for evil, that's not God. The power in my will to choose is good too, and God gave me that. But I can use it wrongly, against God's will.

Sal: All right, but why does God *allow* you to do evil? Why does He allow terrible evils? Why did He allow Hitler to kill six million Jews? Couldn't He perform a miracle and stop it, if He's all-powerful?

Chris: All right, now you're asking the second question: not where evil comes from but where it's going to, what God is doing about it. Are you satisfied with my answer to the first question, before we go on to the second?

Sal: Yes. Evil comes from our free choice. But why did God give us free choice in the first place?

Chris: Because He loved human beings, not robots or puppets.

Sal: All right, but why doesn't He zap all the bad guys now, and heal all the sick people?

Chris: I think it's the same reason our parents don't do our homework for us.

Sal: What do you mean?

Chris: You tell me. Why don't parents do homework for their children?

Sal: I know the answer to that one. If they did, we wouldn't learn anything.

Chris: And that wouldn't be good for students, would it?

Sal: No.

Chris: But doing homework sometimes is a pain, isn't it.

Sal: Yes.

Chris: And parents could take that pain away if they gave their children the answers, couldn't they?

Sal: Yes.

Chris: Are parents evil because they don't take that pain away?

Sal: Of course not. They're good.

Chris: Even though they let their children suffer?

Sal: Yes.

Chris: So just because someone lets you suffer, that doesn't necessarily mean that person is evil.

Sal: No.

Chris: So even though God lets us suffer sometimes, that doesn't mean He's evil either.

Sal: Oh. But the sufferings in the world are a lot worse than homework!

Chris: Of course. I just wanted to show you that someone who is good and loves you could still let you suffer sometimes.

Sal: But why does God let so *much* of it go on? A lot of it is terrible suffering. And why does He let good people suffer as much as bad people?

Chris: Those are very hard questions, and I'm afraid I don't know the answer to them.

Sal: Oh.

Chris: I'm sorry to disappoint you, but I told you before that I don't have all the answers. I'll tell you what I know and I'll tell you what I don't know. No faking it.

Sal: Thanks for being honest, anyway. But how can you still believe in a good God if you don't know why He lets people suffer?

Chris: I know *why* He lets people suffer, I just don't know how He figures it all out. He lets people suffer for the same reason He does everything: He loves us.

Sal: How is it love when He lets a young child die of cancer?

Chris: I don't know. If I knew all the answers to questions like that, I wouldn't have to believe Him. He asks us to trust Him, even when we don't understand.

Sal: I don't understand how you can take such a passive attitude. Just trust God no matter what?

Chris: Oh, we don't take a passive attitude toward evil. We

fight it, in ourselves and in the world (though the weapons we use aren't guns). The most important question about evil is not where it came from but what to do about it, and the answer is to fight it. That's not passive. That's active.

Sal. But where is God in this?

Chris: He didn't originate evil, and He's fighting against it with us, *in* us, even. We're fighting for Him when we fight disease, or prejudice, or tyranny.

Sal: All right, you've kept God *good*, but if He has to fight evil He can't be all-powerful.

Chris: I know for sure that God is all good. I also see that—in Jesus. I believe God is also all-powerful. But I don't see that power, even in Jesus. He died too, and that didn't look like power. But He also rose from the dead, and that was a kind of sign and a promise that God can do anything and that He will conquer all evil in the end.

Sal: Meanwhile, here we are up to our necks in it. Why doesn't He just clean up all the evil now?

Chris: Because He wants *us* to do it. That's part of growing up: doing things for yourself. He's a good Father; He doesn't do everything for His children, even though He can.

Sal: Do you believe He will wipe out all evil in the end?

Chris: Yes. He has told us that. It's in the Bible.

Sal: Why does He wait? Why can't we be at the end now?

Chris: We're in time, like being somewhere in a story that takes time to get to the end. You're asking why we're in the middle of the story now and not at the end. But you have to go through the middle to get to the end, just because it's a story. Every story takes time. You're asking God to create a world without time, a story that gets to the end right away.

Sal: I still feel resentment and hate when I see terribly unjust things happen. I want to blame God even though I don't believe in God.

Chris: But if you blame God, you blame our only hope for conquering evil in the end. He's on our side. He hates evil too. The Bible is full of that. That's why He's so insistent about His laws.

Sal: I think you're just leaping in the dark when you believe in a good God who's going to conquer all evil in the end. That sounds too good to be true. I want to see more evidence before I make that leap. It's hard to trust a God who lets His world get so bad.

Chris: I agree.

Sal: What? I thought you were such a strong believer.

Chris: I do believe. But you're right that it's hard to trust God sometimes, when things go very wrong. It's like a dog trusting a hunter who's trying to get him out of a bear trap; the only way to do that is to push the dog *into* the trap farther first, and that doesn't look like something good. It also hurts. But it's really the best thing for the dog. He can't see that. He just has to trust the hunter.

Sal: That's a nice analogy, but it's not like that with us and God. We don't see any hunter getting us out of the trap of evil.

Chris: Yes we do: Jesus Christ. He came right down into our trap and died to free us. The One Who asks us to trust Him to solve the problem of evil already did the greatest thing to conquer it. He suffered every kind of evil with us. He was hated by the people He loved. He was nailed to a cross, and died. He even felt His Father leave Him horribly alone on the cross, when He said, "My God, my God, why have You forsaken Me?" *That's* evil. All the evil in the world is there, and there He is in the middle of it. You think of God up in Heaven controlling things down here and you wonder why He doesn't do a better job. You wonder if He really cares, and how He can be good if He just stays there and turns away and lets terrible things happen. But it's not like that. He didn't stay away. He came down into evil. That's the Christian answer to the problem of evil: not a tricky argument, but Christ on the cross, God on our side, the side of the innocent sufferer. How can you resent a God like *that*?

Sal: I was thinking of the far away God.

Chris: It *would* be hard to trust a God like that. No, that's not our God. If you want to know what God is like, look at Jesus.

Sal: Now that's a whole new question. I can certainly love and admire Jesus. But Jesus was a man. How can a man be God?

Chris: You have a great way of asking all the good questions. Let's look at that one tomorrow.

Sal: It's a date.

Questions

1. If God is good, where did evil come from?
2. What does Chris say is the most important question about evil?
3. Why doesn't God simply take care of the problem of evil right now?
4. How does Chris use the analogy of the bear trap? What is the point?
5. If you were involved in this dialogue, what questions would you like to ask Chris?

The Why of Suffering

Nicholas Wolterstorff

Philosopher Nicholas Wolterstorff's son Eric was 25 when he slipped and fell to his death in an Austrian mountain climbing accident. In memory of Eric, Wolterstorff wrote Lament for a Son, *from which this selection is excerpted. Wolterstorff grieves through these words, but he also comes to a fresh and hope-filled understanding of the meaning of suffering in this world: "God is not only the God of the sufferers but the God who suffers."*

Born on a snowy night in New Haven, he died twenty-five years later on a snowy slope in the Kaisergebirger. Tenderly we laid him in warm June earth. Willows were releasing their seeds of puffy white, blanketing the ground.

I catch myself: Was it *him* we laid in the earth? I had touched his cheek. Its cold still hardness pushed me back. Death, I knew, was cold. And death was still. But nobody had mentioned that all the softness went out. His spirit had departed and taken along the warmth and activity and, yes, the softness. *He* was gone. "Eric, where are you?" But I am not very good at separating person from body. Maybe that comes with practice. The red hair, the dimples, the chipmunky look—that *was* Eric. . . .

The call came at 3:30 on that Sunday afternoon, a bright sunny day. We had just sent a younger brother off to the plane to be with him for the summer.

"Mr. Wolterstorff?"

"Yes."

"Is this Eric's father?"

"Yes."

"Mr. Wolterstorff, I must give you some bad news."

"Yes."

"Eric has been climbing in the mountains and has had an accident."

"Yes."

"Eric has had a serious accident."

"Yes."

"Mr. Wolterstorff, I must tell you, Eric is dead. Mr. Wolterstorff, are you there? You must come at once! Mr. Wolterstorff, Eric is dead."

For three seconds I felt the peace of resignation: arms extended, limp son in hand, peacefully offering him to someone—Someone. Then the pain—cold burning pain. . . .

A friend remarked after the funeral that what he had seen there was the endurance of faith. He added that this is the message of the book of Job. I think he was right about both.

The only thing that angered me in what people offered was a small book someone gave me written by a father whose son had also been killed in a mountaineering accident. The writer said that in his church on the Sunday before his son's death, they had read Psalm 18. He now interpreted verse 36 as speaking to him:

Thou didst give a wide place for my steps under me,
and my foot did not slip.

His son's foot had not slipped. *God* had shaken the mountain. God had decided that it was time for him to come home.

I find this pious attitude deaf to the message of the Christian gospel. Death is here understood as a normal instrument of God's dealing with us. "You there have lived out the years I've planned for you, so I'll just shake the mountain a bit. All of you there, I'll send some starlings into the engine of your plane. And as for you there, a stroke while running will do nicely."

The Bible speaks instead of God's *overcoming* death. Paul

calls it the last great enemy to be overcome. God is appalled by death. My pain over my son's death is shared by *his* pain over my son's death. And, yes, I share in his pain over *his* son's death.

Seeing God as the agent of death is one way of fitting together into a rational pattern God, ourselves, and death. There are other ways. One of these has been explored in a book by Rabbi Kushner: God too is pained by death, more even than you and I are; but there's nothing much he can do about it.

I cannot fit it all together by saying, "He did it," but neither can I do so by saying, "There was nothing he could do about it." I cannot fit it together at all. I can only, with Job, endure. I do not know why God did not prevent Eric's death. To live without the answer is precarious. It's hard to keep one's footing.

Job's friends tried out on him their answer. "God did it, Job; he was the agent of your children's death. He did it because of some wickedness in you; he did it to punish you. Nothing indeed in your public life would seem to merit such retribution; it must then be something in your private inner life. Tell us what it is, Job. Confess."

The writer of Job refuses to say that God views the lives and deaths of children as cats-o'-nine-tails with which to lacerate parents.

I have no explanation. I can do nothing else than endure in the face of this deepest and most painful of mysteries. I believe in God the Father Almighty, maker of heaven and earth and resurrecter of Jesus Christ. I also believe that my son's life was cut off in its prime. I cannot fit these pieces together. I am at a loss. I have read the theodicies produced to justify the ways of God to man. I find them unconvincing. To the most agonized question I have ever asked I do not know the answer. I do not know why God would watch him fall. I do not know why God would watch me wounded. I cannot even guess.

C.S. Lewis, writing about the death of his wife, was plainly angry with God. He, Lewis, deserved something better than to be treated so shabbily. I am not angry but baffled and hurt. My wound is an unanswered question. The wounds of all humanity are an unanswered question. . . .

I have come to see that the Christian gospel tells us more of the meaning of sin than of suffering. Of sin it says that its root lies not in God but in the will of the human being. It is true that an inclination toward lovelessness and injustice is now mysteriously perpetuated down through the generations. But it remains an inclination, not a necessity. Sin belongs to us. To this the gospel adds that our lovelessness pains God; it grieves him. And then the good news: God's response to this pain is forgiveness—not avenging fury but forgiveness. Jesus Christ is the announcement: the Master of the Universe forgives.

To the "why" of suffering we get no firm answer. Of course some suffering is easily seen to be the result of our sin: war, assault, poverty amidst plenty, the hurtful word. And maybe some is chastisement. But not all. The meaning of the remainder is not told us. It eludes us. Our net of meaning is too small. There's more to our suffering than our guilt.

"Truly, you are a God who hides yourself, O
God of Israel, the Savior" (Isa. 45:15).
    "A religion which does not affirm that God is hidden is not true. *Vere tu es Deus absconditus*—truly you are a hidden God" (Pascal).
    Perhaps it has been a mistake to think that God reveals himself. He speaks, yes. But as he speaks, he hides. His face he does not show us.

Why don't you just scrap this God business, says one of my bitter suffering friends. It's a rotten world, you and I have been shafted, and that's that.

I'm pinned down. When I survey this gigantic intricate world, I cannot believe that it just came about. I do not mean that I have some good arguments for its being made and that I believe in the arguments. I mean that this conviction wells up irresistibly within me when I contemplate the world. The experiment of trying to abolish it does not work. When looking at the heavens, I cannot manage to believe that they do not declare the glory of God. When looking at the earth, I cannot bring off the attempt to believe that it does not display his handiwork.

And when I read the New Testament and look into the material surrounding it, I am convinced that the man Jesus of Nazareth was raised from the dead. In that, I see the sign that he was more than a prophet. He was the Son of God.

Faith is a footbridge that you don't know will hold you up over the chasm until you're forced to walk out onto it. I'm standing there now, over the chasm. I inspect the bridge. Am I deluded in believing that in God the question shouted out by the wounds of the world has its answer? Am I deluded in believing that someday I will know the answer? Am I deluded in believing that once I know the answer, I will see that love has conquered?

I cannot dispel the sense of conducting my inspection in the presence of the Creating/Resurrecting One.

With every fiber of my being I long to talk with Eric again. When I mentioned this to someone, she asked what I would say. I don't know. Maybe I would just blurt out something silly. That would be good enough for a beginning. We could take it from there. Every day I wonder, and some days I doubt, whether that talk will ever take place. But then comes that insistent voice: "Remember, I made all this and raised my own son from the dead, so I can also. . . . "

"I know, I know. But why don't you raise mine now? Why did you ever let him die? If creation took just six days, why does re-creation take so agonizingly long? If your conquest of primeval chaos went so quickly, why must your conquest of sin and death and suffering be so achingly slow?"

When I say my first words to Eric, then God's reign will be here. . . .

How is faith to endure, O God, when you allow all this

scraping and tearing on us? You have allowed rivers of blood to flow, mountains of suffering to pile up, sobs to become humanity's song—all without lifting a finger that we could see. You have allowed bonds of love beyond number to be painfully snapped. If you have not abandoned us, explain yourself.

We strain to hear. But instead of hearing an answer we catch sight of God himself scraped and torn. Through our tears we see the tears of God.

A new and more disturbing question now arises: Why do you permit yourself to suffer, O God? If the death of the devout costs you dear (Psalm 116:15), why do you permit it? Why do you not grasp joy?

For a long time I knew that God is not the impassive, unresponsive, unchanging being portrayed by the classical theologians. I knew of the pathos of God. I knew of God's response of delight and of his response of displeasure. But strangely, his suffering I never saw before.

God is not only the God of the sufferers but the God who suffers. The pain and fallenness of humanity have entered into his heart. Through the prism of my tears I have seen a suffering God.

It is said of God that no one can behold his face and live. I always thought this meant that no one could see his splendor and live. A friend said perhaps it meant that no one could see his sorrow and live. Or perhaps his sorrow is splendor.

And great mystery: to redeem our brokenness and lovelessness the God who suffers with us did not strike some mighty blow of power but sent his beloved son to suffer *like* us, through his suffering to redeem us from suffering and evil.

Instead of explaining our suffering God shares it.

But I never saw it. Though I confessed that the man of sorrows was God himself, I never saw the God of sorrows. Though I confessed that the man bleeding on the cross was the redeeming God, I never saw God himself on the cross, blood from sword and thorn and nail dripping healing into the world's wounds.

What does this mean for life, that God suffers? I'm only beginning to learn. When we think of God the Creator, then we naturally see the rich and powerful of the earth as his closest image. But when we hold steady before us the sight of God the Redeemer redeeming from sin and suffering by suffering, then perhaps we must look elsewhere for earth's closest icon. Where? Perhaps to the face of that woman with soup tin in hand and bloated child at side. Perhaps that is why Jesus said that inasmuch as we show love to such a one, we show love to him.

Made in the image of God: That is how the biblical writers describe us. To be human is to be an icon of God. This glory is one we cannot lose. It can be increased or diminished, though; our imaging can be closer or farther, more glorious or less. Authentic life is to image God ever more closely by becoming like Jesus Christ, the express image of the Father.

In what respects do we mirror God? In our knowledge. In our love. In our justice. In our sociality. In our creativity. These are the answers the Christian tradition offers us.

One answer rarely finds its way onto the list: in our suffering. Perhaps the thought is too appalling. Do we also mirror God in suffering? Are we to mirror him ever more closely in suffering? Was it meant that we should be icons in suffering? Is it our glory to suffer? . . .

God is love. That is why he suffers. To love our suffering sinful world is to suffer. God so suffered for the world that he gave up his only Son to suffering. The one who does not see God's suffering does not see his love. God is suffering love.

So suffering is down at the center of things, deep down where the meaning is. Suffering is the meaning of our world. For Love is the meaning. And Love suffers. The tears of God are the meaning of history.

But mystery remains. Why isn't Love-*without*-suffering the meaning of things? Why is *suffering*-Love the meaning? Why does God endure his suffering? Why does he not at once relieve his agony by relieving ours?

We're in it together, God and we, together in the history of our world. The history of our world is the history of our suffering together. Every act of evil extracts a tear from God, every plunge into anguish extracts a sob from God. But also the history of our world is the history of our deliverance together. God's work to release himself from his suffering is his work to deliver the world from its agony; our struggle for joy and justice is our struggle to relieve God's sorrow.

When God's cup of suffering is full, our world's redemption is fulfilled. Until justice and peace embrace, God's dance of joy is delayed.

The bells for the feast of divine joy are the bells for the shalom of the world.

Questions

1. The pious suggestion that God caused Eric's death makes Wolterstorff angry. Explain why the author rejects this attitude.
2. According to the writer, what causes God to suffer?
3. Why is it such a revelation to Wolterstorff to discover that God suffers, too?

Do You Really Expect Me to Believe in Miracles?

Atheist View

H.A. Gurney

This selection appeared originally as a letter to the editor of
New Humanist *magazine. The writer is an atheist who
believes that it is time for everyone to grow up and get rid of
"those fantastic stories" about Jesus' miracles, resurrection,
and so on. Just the "simple idea" of a man like Jesus has been
enough to produce many good works as well as many cathedrals erected in his honor.*

As an out-and-out atheist I find it impossible to believe that
some "Being" (or a trinity of them) created the universe. But I
find it perfectly understandable that primitive man should
have done so and his need for a God (but which later he unfor-
tunately created in his own image).

At the infant Sunday school I attended I always found help
and comfort (and still do) from what I was taught there about
Jesus Christ and his love and compassion for all and courage
in proclaiming it in a cruel age. But surely it is high time that
we all "grew up" (and particularly those who still wear their

"souls" on their sleeves) and discarded those fantastic stories about his miracles and resurrection and divine parentage and messiah-ship (which may have been foisted on him against his will), and finally leading to his terrible death on the cross. And even if it could be proved that Jesus never really existed, just the simple idea of such a man and his gospel of love has been enough to produce many "good works"—as well, of course, as the great cathedrals which men have erected and still maintain in his honour.

Questions

1. What is the writer's worldview?
2. How does the writer explain the existence of the universe?
3. What does he call miracles? Why?
4. Does he believe that there is a personal God?

Why I Am An Agnostic

Clarence Darrow

In this essay Clarence Darrow attacks several doctrines of the Christian faith, including the origin of the universe, the nature of the soul, miracles, sin, and the virgin birth of Jesus. Miracles, he says, are nothing less than violations of a natural law. We have no business believing in miracles, unless we understand all natural laws. To do otherwise is inconsistent with knowledge and logic.

An agnostic is a doubter. The word is generally applied to those who doubt the verity of accepted religious creeds of faiths. Everyone is an agnostic as to the beliefs or creeds they do not accept. Catholics are agnostic to the Protestant creeds, and the Protestants are agnostic to the Catholic creed. Anyone who thinks is an agnostic about something, otherwise he must believe that he is possessed of all knowledge. And the proper place for such a person is in the madhouse or the home for the feeble-minded. In a popular way, in the western world, an agnostic is one who doubts or disbelieves the main tenets of the Christian faith.

I would say that belief in at least three tenets is necessary to the faith of a Christian: a belief in God, a belief in immortality, and a belief in a supernatural book. Various Christian sects require much more, but it is difficult to imagine that one could be a Christian, under any intelligent meaning of the word, with less. Yet there are some people who claim to be Christians who do not accept the literal interpretation of all the Bible, and who give more credence to some portions of the book than to others.

I am an agnostic as to the question of God. I think that it is impossible for the human mind to believe in an object or thing unless it can form a mental picture of such object or thing. Since man ceased to worship openly an anthropomorphic god and talked vaguely and not intelligently about some force in the universe, higher than man, that is responsible for the existence of man and the universe, he cannot be said to believe in God. One cannot believe in a force excepting as a force that pervades matter and is not an individual entity. To believe in a thing, an image of the thing must be stamped on the mind. If one is asked if he believes in such an animal as a camel, there immediately arises in his mind an image of the camel. This image has come from experience or knowledge of the animal gathered in some way or other. No such image comes, or can come, with the idea of a god who is described as a force.

Man has always speculated upon the origin of the universe, including himself. I feel, with Herbert Spencer, that whether the universe had an origin—and if it had—what the origin is will never be known by man. The Christian says that the universe could not make itself; that there must have been some higher power to call it into being. Christians have been obsessed for many years by Paley's argument that if a person passing through a desert should find a watch and examine its spring, its hands, its case and its crystal, he would at once be satisfied that some intelligent being capable of design had made the watch. No doubt this is true. No civilized man would question that someone made the watch. The reason he would not doubt it is because he is familiar with watches and other appliances made by man. The savage was once unfamiliar with a watch and would have had no idea upon the subject. There are plenty of crystals and rocks of natural formation that are as intricate as a watch, but even to intelligent man they carry no implication that some intelligent power must have made them. They carry no such implication because no one has any knowledge or experience of someone having made these natural objects which everywhere abound.

To say that God made the universe gives us no explanation of the beginnings of things. If we are told that God made the universe, the question immediately arises: Who made God?

Did he always exist, or was there some power back of that? Did he create matter out of nothing, or is his existence coextensive with matter? The problem is still there. What is the origin of it all? If, on the other hand, one says that the universe was not made by God, that it always existed, he has the same difficulty to confront. To say that the universe was here last year, or millions of years ago, does not explain its origin. This is still a mystery. As to the question of the origin of things, man can only wonder and doubt and guess.

As to the existence of the soul, all people may either believe or disbelieve. Everyone knows the origin of the human being. They know that it came from a single cell in the body of the mother, and that the cell was one out of ten thousand in the mother's body. Before gestation the cell must have been fertilized by a spermatozoön from the body of the father. This was one out of perhaps a billion spermatozoa that was the capacity of the father. When the cell is fertilized a chemical process begins. The cell divides and multiplies and increases into millions of cells, and finally a child is born. Cells die and are born during the life of the individual until they finally drop apart, and this is death.

If there is a soul, what is it, and where did it come from, and where does it go? Can anyone who is guided by his reason possibly imagine a soul independent of a body, or the place of its residence, or the character of it, or anything concerning it? If man is justified in any belief or disbelief on any subject, he is warranted in the disbelief in a soul. Not one scrap of evidence exists to prove any such impossible thing.

Many Christians base the belief of a soul and God upon the Bible. Strictly speaking, there is no such book. To make the Bible, sixty-six books are bound into one volume. These books are written by many people at different times, and no one knows the time or the identity of any author. Some of the books were written by several authors at various times. These books contain all sorts of contradictory concepts of life and morals and the origin of things. Between the first and the last nearly a thousand years intervened, a longer time than has passed since the discovery of America by Columbus.

When I was a boy the theologians used to assert that the proof of the divine inspiration of the Bible rested on miracles and prophecies. But a miracle means a violation of a natural law, and there can be no proof imagined that could be sufficient to show the violation of a natural law; even though proof seemed to show violation, it would hardly show that we were not acquainted with all natural laws. One believes in the truthfulness of a man because of his long experience with the man, and because the man has always told a consistent story. But no man has told so consistent a story as nature.

If one should say that the sun did not rise, to use the ordinary expression, on the day before, his hearer would not believe it, even though he had slept all day and knew that his informant was a man of the strictest veracity. He would not believe it because the story is inconsistent with the conduct of the sun in all the ages past.

Primitive and even civilized people have grown so accustomed to believing in miracles that they often attribute the simplest manifestations of nature to agencies of which they know nothing. They do this when the belief is utterly inconsistent with knowledge and logic. They believe in old miracles and new ones. Preachers pray for rain, knowing full well that no such prayer was ever answered. When a politician is sick, they pray to God to cure him, and the politician almost invariably dies. The modern clergyman who prays for rain and for the health of the politician is no more intelligent in this matter than the primitive man who saw a separate miracle in the rising and setting of the sun, in the birth of an individual, in the growth of a plant, in the stroke of lightning, in the flood, in every manifestation of nature and life.

As to prophecies, intelligent writers gave them up long ago. In all prophecies facts are made to suit the prophecy, or the prophecy was made after the facts, or the events have no relation to the prophecy. Weird and strange and unreasonable interpretations are used to explain simple statements, that a prophecy may be claimed.

Can any rational person believe that the Bible is anything but a human document? We now know pretty well where the various books came from, and about when they were written. We know that they were written by human beings who had no knowledge of science, little knowledge of life, and were influenced by the barbarous morality of primitive times, and were grossly ignorant of most things that men know today. For instance, Genesis says that God made the earth, and he made the sun to light the day and the moon to light the night, and in one clause disposes of the stars by saying that "he made the stars also." This was plainly written by someone who had no conception of the stars. Man, by the aid of his telescope, has looked out into the heavens and found stars whose diameter is as great as the distance between the earth and the sun. We know that the universe is filled with stars and suns and planets and systems. Every new telescope looking further into the heavens only discovers more and more worlds and suns and systems in the endless reaches of space. The men who wrote Genesis believed, of course, that this tiny speck of mud that we call earth was the center of the universe, the only world in space, and made for man, who was the only being worth considering. These men believed that the stars were only a little way above the earth, and were set in the firmament for man to look at, and for nothing else. Everyone today knows that this conception is not true.

The origin of the human race is not as blind a subject as it once was. Let alone God creating Adam out of hand, from the dust of the earth, does anyone believe that Eve was made from Adam's rib—that the snake walked and spoke in the Garden of Eden—that he tempted Eve to persuade Adam to eat an apple, and that it is on that account that the whole human race was doomed to hell—that for four thousand years there was no chance for any human to be saved, though none of them had anything whatever to do with the temptation; and that finally men were saved only through God's son dying for them, and that unless human beings believed this silly, impossible and wicked story they were doomed to hell? Can anyone with intelligence really believe that a child born today should be doomed because the snake tempted Eve and Eve tempted Adam? To believe that is not God-worship; it is devil-worship.

Can anyone call this scheme of creation and damnation moral? It defies every principle of morality, as man conceives morality. Can anyone believe today that the whole world was destroyed by flood, save only Noah and his family and a male and female of each species of animal that entered the Ark? There are almost a million species of insects alone. How did Noah match these up and make sure of getting male and female to reproduce life in the world after the flood had spent its force? And why should all the lower animals have been destroyed? Were they included in the sinning of man? This is a story which could not beguile a fairly bright child of five years of age today.

Do intelligent people believe that the various languages spoken by man on earth came from the confusion of tongues at the Tower of Babel, some four thousand years ago? Human languages were dispersed all over the face of the earth long before that time. Evidences of civilizations are in existence now that were old long before the date the romancers fix for the building of the tower, and even before the date claimed for the flood.

Do Christians believe that Joshua made the sun stand still, so that the day could be lengthened, that a battle might be finished? What kind of person wrote that story, and what did he know about astronomy? It is perfectly plain that the author thought that the earth was the center of the universe and stood still in the heavens, and that the sun either went around it or was pulled across its path each day, and that the stopping of the sun would lengthen the day. We know now that had the sun stopped when Joshua commanded it, and had it stood still until now, it would not have lengthened the day. We know that the day is determined by the rotation of the earth upon its axis, and not by the movement of the sun. Everyone knows that this story simply is not true, and not many even pretend to believe this childish fable.

What of the tale of Balaam's asses speaking to him, probably in Hebrew? Is it true, or is it a fable? Many asses have spoken, and doubtless some in Hebrew, but they have not been that breed of asses. Is salvation to depend on a belief in a monstrosity like this?

Above all the rest, would any human being today believe that a child was born without a father? Yet this story was not at all unreasonable in the ancient world; at least three or four miraculous births are recorded in the Bible, including John the Baptist and Samson. Immaculate conceptions were common in the Roman world at the time and at the place where Christianity really had its nativity. Women were taken to the temples to be inoculated of God so that their sons might be heroes, which meant, generally, wholesale butchers. Julius Caesar was a miraculous conception—indeed, they were common all over the world. How many miraculous-birth stories is a Christian now expected to believe?

In the days of the formation of the Christian religion, disease meant the possession of human beings by devils. Christ cured a sick man by casting out the devils, who ran into the swine, and the swine ran into the sea. Is there any question but what that was simply the attitude and belief of a primitive people? Does anyone believe that sickness means the possession of the body by devils, and that the devils must be cast out of the human being that he may be cured? Does anyone believe that a dead person can come to life? The miracles recorded in the Bible are not the only instances of dead men coming to life. All over the world one finds testimony of such miracles: miracles which no person is expected to believe, unless it is his kind of miracle. Still at Lourdes today, and all over the present world, from New York to Los Angeles and up and down the lands, people believe in miraculous occurrences, and even in the return of the dead. Superstition is everywhere prevalent in the world. It has been so from the beginning, and most likely will be so unto the end.

The reasons for agnosticism are abundant and compelling. Fantastic and foolish and impossible consequences are freely claimed for the belief in religion. All the civilization of any period is put down as a result of religion. All the cruelty and error and ignorance of the period has no relation to religion. The truth is that the origin of what we call civilization is not due to religion but to skepticism. So long as men accepted miracles without question, so long as they believed in original sin and the road to salvation, so long as they believed in hell where man would be kept for eternity on account of Eve, there was no reason whatever for civilization; life was short, and eternity was long, and the business of life was preparation of eternity.

When every event was a miracle, when there was no order or system or law, there was no occasion for studying any subject, or being interested in anything excepting a religion which took care of the soul. As man doubted the primitive conceptions about religion, and no longer accepted the literal, miraculous teachings of ancient books, he set himself to understand nature. We no longer cure disease by casting out devils. Since that time, men have studied the human body, have built hospitals and treated illness in a scientific way. Science is responsible for the building of railroads and bridges, of steamships, of telegraph lines, of cities, towns, large buildings and small, plumbing and sanitation, of the food supply, and the countless thousands of useful things that we now deem necessary to life. Without skepticism and doubt, none of these things could have been given to the world.

The fear of God is not the beginning of wisdom. The fear of God is the death of wisdom. Skepticism and doubt lead to study and investigation, and investigation is the beginning of wisdom.

The modern world is the child of doubt and inquiry, as the ancient world the child of fear and faith.

Questions

1. According to Darrow, what is an agnostic? Why does he say it is impossible to believe in God? How does he characterize Christianity?

2. For Darrow, what is "the beginning of wisdom"? Why does he say that?

3. Why do you think some people are agnostics concerning Christianity? Does it require more or less faith to be an agnostic than to be a Christian? Give reasons for your answer.

Miracles

Peter Kreeft

Sal and Chris are in another head-to-head discussion. This time it's about miracles. Chris deftly defends the reality and believability of miracles. Chris makes several points, including these: (1) miracles are not God's afterthoughts; (2) miracles are signs that reveal God; (3) miracles do not violate the laws of nature; and (4) they are supported by a solid foundation of "historical evidence."

Sal: You know, Chris, I'm really impressed by how everything you believe is tied together. I can't believe all the things Jesus said, as you do, because I can't believe Jesus was God. And I can't believe Jesus was God because I can't believe he rose from the dead. And I can't believe that because I can't believe in miracles.

Chris: So let's talk about miracles. I respect your mind, Sal. You see how it all hangs together. Some people try to pick and choose what parts of Christianity they "feel comfortable with," as if Christians offered Christianity to the world as a comfort pill instead of as truth.

Sal: No Christianity without miracles, eh?

Chris: No such thing. Drop the miraculous element and you get a totally different religion.

Sal: Why?

Chris: Because everything distinctive to Christianity is a miracle. Creation, Jewish prophecies of the Messiah, the Incarnation of God in Jesus, Jesus' own miracles, His resurrection from the grave, and His return at the end of time: all the important events in the story are miracles. And Christianity is essentially a story, "good news."

Sal: But other religions have miracle stories too, don't they?

Chris: Many others do, yes. But if you drop them out, the essential points remain intact in Islam and Confucianism and Taoism and Buddhism, and even Hinduism.

Sal: What about Judaism?

Chris: The Hebrew Scriptures are part of the Christian Scriptures, and they're full of miracles. It's the same God, after all, that Judaism and Christianity are about, the same God that the Old Testament and the New Testament are about.

Sal: This God is supposed to be perfect, right?

Chris: Right.

Sal: And he's supposed to have created the universe, right?

Chris: Right.

Sal: Well, why would a perfect God create a universe with so many imperfections in it that he has to perform miracles in it? That's like a plumber putting in a leaky pipe and then coming back to patch it up over and over again.

Chris: Oh, but miracles aren't leak-patches, not after-thoughts. They're master-strokes of his art. They *fit*.

Sal: I don't see that. If the laws of nature are perfect, why does God make exceptions to them by miracles?

Chris: For the same reason any great artist makes exceptions to his general rules. Those rules aren't absolute. Do you really think the final, absolute rules of God's work are the little regularities our science has discovered so far?

Sal: Why not?

Chris: That's like thinking you understand a great painting because you've counted the little dots of color. A good artist is always wiser than you, and he surprises you. If you have him all figured out, then he's a little artist, not a great one. And God is a very great one.

Sal: So it's blind faith, this belief in miracles.

Chris: No indeed. After you get over the surprise, you understand it a little. After the miracles happen, you see their point. They're signs. The word for "miracle" in New Testament Greek means "sign." They point beyond themselves. They teach a lesson, reveal God.

Sal: I like that. You don't need the miracle itself, then.

Chris: You do. If a sign weren't real, how could it teach you? First you look at it, then you look along it.

Sal: OK, so miracles are to teach us something. What?

Chris: What God is like. Miracles of healing show us that God is a God of life and health, and wants us happy. They show us that God has both love and power, that those two things that are so often tragically separated in our lives are perfectly united in God. That's just one thing miracles teach us. There are more.

Sal: I have a problem with that—with God teaching us by miracles. They seem unworthy of what you mean by God.

Chris: Why?

Sal: They seem so crude, so primitive. Why should God need to put on a big show like that? It's . . . well, undignified.

Chris: If you saw one, would that help you believe?

Sal: Of course.

Chris: Then that's why God stoops from His dignity. He's a good teacher. He comes down to our level. He's no snob.

Sal: But people shouldn't need crude power displays to believe.

Chris: Perhaps not, but they do. *You* do, for one. You just said so yourself

Sal: I? When?

Chris: When I asked, If you saw a miracle, would that help you believe? and you said yes.

Sal: Oh. You got me there. But even if miracles would be proper for God, they just don't happen.

Chris: That's what you *believe*, isn't it?

Sal: Yes.

Chris: Well, I think on this question of miracles you're the one who goes by faith and I'm the one who goes by reason and scientific evidence.

Sal: What? Why do you say that?

Chris: Because I have a lot of historical evidence on my side, and you have nothing but your unsupported conviction that "miracles just don't happen."

Sal: Wait a minute. I've got evidence too. I've heard of fake miracles, and I think you have too. If some were fake, why couldn't all be fake? We can be fooled, you know, just as we are by stage magicians.

Chris: That's like arguing that since you've seen some counterfeit money, why couldn't all money be counterfeit? A few fakes don't disprove the genuine article. If anything, they're a clue that there *is* a genuine article there to be imitated.

Sal: Well, I never saw any miracles.

Chris: And therefore you don't believe in them?

Sal: Right.

Chris: Then you'd better throw away your textbooks.

Sal: What do you mean?

Chris: Why do you believe your science or history or geography books? They tell you things you didn't see, like electrons and Caesar and Australia.

Sal: But people have seen those things. Reliable people. Many people.

Chris: And people have seen miracles. Reliable people. Many people.

Sal: No. The people who claim to see miracles are not reliable people, like scientists and historians.

Chris: Why aren't they reliable?

Sal: Why, because they claim to see miracles, of course!

Chris: Have you every heard of "arguing in a circle?"

Sal: Oh. That *was* arguing in a circle, wasn't it?

Chris: Yes. It was just as silly as saying you don't believe in Australia even though many people say they've seen it, because those people must be unreliable, and then saying the reason they must be unreliable is because they say they've seen Australia.

Sal: But what solid historical evidence is there for miracles?

Chris: Plenty. Have you ever looked?

Sal: No.

Chris: Why not?

Sal: It would be a waste of time.

Chris: Because you know that miracles don't happen?

Sal: That's another circle, isn't it? Well, I *do* know miracles don't happen, because they'd violate the laws of nature.

You can't believe in miracles and science at the same time.

Chris: Yes you can. Let me try to explain. Would a presidential pardon to a criminal violate the laws of the court? Would a gift of extra money violate the laws of accounting? Would a hand adding food to a fish bowl violate the ecology of the fish bowl?

Sal: No, they just add to it.

Chris: Then why would miracles violate the laws of nature? They just *add* something. In fact, miracles *presuppose* the laws of nature. If there were no laws of nature, there couldn't be any distinction between natural events and miraculous events.

Sal: I see. But nature can't make miracles, can it?

Chris: No.

Sal: So it would have to be God who does miracles.

Chris: Right.

Sal: Well, then, how can human beings perform miracles? There are a lot of stories about them. Mustn't they all be false?

Chris: No human being can perform a miracle. But God can perform one through a human being as his instrument. A shovel can't dig a hole by itself, but I can use one to dig a hole.

Sal: I see. Well, here's what I think about those stories. They came from an age of ignorance of science and the laws of nature. What people in the past took to be miracles we can now explain scientifically. People came to believe in miracles only because they didn't know that clouds, not Zeus, made thunder, and that tides, not Neptune, made tidal waves.

Chris: But miracle stories don't just come from the past. There are thousands of well-documented miracles today too.

Sal: Well, science will explain them too one day. What one age thinks of as miraculous, the next age explains by science.

Chris: You mean modern science says virgin births and resurrections from the grave and walking on water and through walls and feeding five thousand people from five loaves and two fishes isn't miraculous?

Sal: Some day science will explain them too, if they really happened.

Chris: That's quite a faith you have. Science hasn't explained away a single real miracle in hundreds of years, yet you believe that in the future it will explain away *all* miracles. You have as much faith in science as I have in God, it seems.

Sal: Science has explained some miracles.

Chris: Name one.

Sal: The parting of the Red Sea. A wind did that, not God.

Chris: Where did you get that idea?

Sal: Science, of course.

Chris: Wrong. You got it from the Bible.

Sal: What?

Chris. *Exodus* says it was a wind. But it also says it was God: "God raised up a wind."

Sal: Then that *wasn't* a miracle.

Chris: Perhaps not. But it was Providence: perfect timing.

Sal: Well, what about the virgin birth?

Chris: What about it?

Sal: Today we know all the details of the birth process. In an age of ignorance they could believe in a virgin birth. But no longer.

Chris: Really? You mean Mary and Joseph didn't know how babies are made? Come on now! What kind of chronological snob are you?

Sal: What's a chronological snob?

Chris: Someone who looks down his nose not at other classes of people in the present but at all classes of people in the past. Someone who dismisses an idea not because it's proved to be untrue but just because more people in the past believed it than in the present. Someone who asks of an idea not whether it's *true*, but whether it's *new*.

Sal: But they *didn't* know much science.

Chris: They didn't know all the details of how pregnancy worked inside a woman. But they certainly knew how it originated outside! A virgin birth is just as miraculous in 2000 B.C. as in A.D. 2, and just as miraculous in A.D. 2 as in A.D. 2000. You still haven't found a miracle that science has explained away.

Sal: What about faith healings? Modern psychology calls them psychosomatic. Our own mind can heal our body: the power of mind over matter.

Chris: Once again, that idea is taught in the Bible too. Jesus often says, "Your faith has healed you." Not all healings are miraculous. Many are psychosomatic. And the ancients knew at least as much about that as we do: about the power of mind over matter.

Sal: So, *all* healings are psychosomatic then. You don't need God to explain them.

Chris: Not all. Raising the dead isn't psychosomatic. Or walking on water. Or feeding five thousand.

Sal: Well, I just don't believe they ever really happened.

Chris: That's an interesting statement about your private feelings, but it doesn't alter the facts, you know. The world doesn't wait for your beliefs to run the way it does.

Sal: Are you making fun of me?

Chris: No. Sorry if I seemed to. But I wanted you to see the point that you haven't given any *evidence,* any reasons for your belief. You go by tender, dreamy feelings—your feelings. I go by hard evidence. You go by your narrow-minded dogma. I have an open mind. Your philosophy doesn't allow you to believe in miracles. Mine does.

Sal: Hey! *I'm* supposed to be the hard-headed, open-minded scientist and *you're* supposed to be the prejudiced dogmatist.

Chris: I think you can see that that labeling itself is a prejudice. If you're open minded enough to see it.

Sal: Hmmm. Most of the miracles you believe in are in the Bible, aren't they?

Chris: Yes. The ones I'm sure of, anyway.

Sal: Then we'd better talk about the Bible next. The main reason I never believed what the Bible said was because it was so full of miracles. Everything hangs together.

Chris: Yes, it does. See you tomorrow.

Questions

1. What makes Christianity unique?
2. How do miracles "fit" into the creation?
3. Why can't science and reason ultimately refute the reality of miracles?

Isn't It Irrational to Believe in Miracles?

Douglas C. Spanner

Douglas C. Spanner answers the question of belief in miracles by asking two others: (1) What does the Bible mean by a "miracle"? (2) Why do miracles constitute a difficulty? With clear answers to those questions and a biblical view of God's relationship to his universe, one can see that there is, indeed, room for both science and miracles from a truly biblical point of view.

No, it isn't. Why not? To answer this adequately there are two subsidiary questions we must first attend to. The first is: What does the Bible mean by a "miracle"? (Naturally it is the biblical usage we must consider, not the popular one.) The second is: Why do miracles constitute a difficulty? When we have considered these we shall be able to see how, in the light of the Bible's revelation of the relationship between God and the world of nature, biblical miracles are not only reasonable but necessary. Let us take these two questions in order.

What does the Bible mean by a miracle?

In the Bible miracles are referred to mainly by three words which some translators have rendered *signs, wonders,* and *mighty works,* the three occurring together in Acts 2:22 RV and 2 Corinthians 12:12 RV, but being of frequent occurrence elsewhere. These three words enable us to see just what the Bible intends to convey.

A miracle is something which by its striking or unusual nature *compels attention* (it is a *wonder*—see for instance the story of Moses in Exodus 3:1-4, or John 12:9 . However, the matter does not end there. If it did there would be little distinction between miracle and magic. Having attracted attention the happening *conveys a message* (it is a *sign*, as emphasized in John 2:11, 3:2 RV); and further, an important feature of the message is that *power is present*, and power of such a quality that it must be recognized as divine (it is a *mighty work*—our word *dynamic* comes from the same Greek root).

In view of all this, and of the biblical teaching that man is in bondage to sin (John 8:34) and on the road to destruction (Matthew 7:13), the role of miracle in the biblical revelation is rather like that of a neon sign reading EMERGENCY EXIT in a building subject to fire. It is designed to arrest attention, and to convey a message which if heeded will lead to life and liberty.

Why do miracles constitute a difficulty?

Undoubtedly in the main they do so because they seem to run counter to the picture of the world which science has given us. This is of a universe which exemplifies fixed laws, such as Newton's laws of motion, or Mendel's laws of heredity. These laws are our ways of expressing a quite fundamental conviction we have formed about Nature, a conviction often stated rather inadequately in the form: "the same physical cause always produces the same physical effect." When we release a stone it *always* falls; when we put a kettle on the gas it *always* grows hotter; when we bring together two suitable pieces of plutonium they *always* explode; and so on.

It is this regular behaviour of Nature that lies at the basis of our success in formulating scientific laws, and so of predicting physical events and harnessing physical forces. And the impressive achievements of science, both on the theoretical and on the practical level, argue in the strongest possible way that the scientist's conviction that Nature is *essentially* law-abiding is a valid one.

Now it is this conviction that a belief in miracles seems to undermine. Stones may usually be expected to fall, but on rather odd occasions they may quite unaccountably do otherwise! Or to take an example with more direct biblical reference, while the principle of the conservation of mass has proved its worth to countless investigators on numberless occasions, it constitutes a foundation much less satisfactory than supposed, for on more than one occasion it has failed, and failed spectacularly (2 Kings 4:1-6; Matthew 16:9-10).

On the face of it, therefore, belief in miracles does seem to put us in the intolerable position of having to question the validity of one of those fundamental principles on which not merely this or that particular scientific theory depends, but the very possibility of *having any science at all*. If Nature is *at rock-bottom* capricious and unpredictable (as miracles seem to suggest), the whole scientific enterprise with its reliance on law-abidingness becomes highly precarious. No wonder many scientists boggle at the miraculous!

The relationship between God and his universe

Before we pass on to see how the Bible provides for the validity of both science and the miraculous we must notice a common view, often held, of the relationship between God and his universe. This view (spoken of as Deism) thinks of God as an expert clockmaker. Having made a superlative mechanism he now leaves it to tick on its own. If it goes wrong he "intervenes" to put it right. It is such an act of intervention that constitutes a miracle.

Now while this view does make some sort of sense of both science and miracle (after all, clocks *do* operate according to very real built-in laws; and yet their escapement mechanism can "slip a cog" and introduce an element of irregularity), it doesn't do anything like justice to the biblical revelation of God as Creator.

The Bible discloses that God is not just a clockmaker (who has given his creation more or less independent existence), but in some respects more like a great conductor of an orchestra on whose continuing activity the steady outpouring of the music depends. On this analogy the creation is like the sounding music. While the clockmaker can withdraw and the clock tick on, the moment the conductor withdraws the music ceases. This is what is meant by saying God is both *immanent* in his creation as well as *transcendent* over it (this view is called Theism); and the Bible very definitely teaches this (see very numerous passages including 2 Corinthians 1:17 RSV; Psalm 104; Matthew 5:45, 6:26, 30, 32—notice the present tenses).

The Bible's provision for the validity of both science and miracles

It is here that a very satisfying possibility exists of doing justice to the well-attested evidence for miracles without endangering the security of scientific foundations. It comes about like this. The Bible regards natural laws as arising not from the perfection of a mechanism (as the Deist does) but from the faithfulness of the Creator. Natural laws are our descriptions of what we observe of his mode of working, and because capriciousness is utterly foreign to God's nature (Malachi 3:6; James 1:17) the validity of Nature's laws is an ultimate one. To depend upon them is not to build in the least on a precarious foundation (see Genesis 8:21-22; Jeremiah 31:35-36). God knows that man's life would be impossible were he not able to rely on Nature; if, for instance, pressure on the pedals of his cycle caused movement in a quite unpredictable direction. Accordingly, in his faithfulness he maintains constant the pattern of his workings in the realm of mechanics, and Newton's laws of motion appear.

But this insistence on the faithfulness of God to man's needs has other implications. What if man is, since his fall (as the Bible asserts), an abnormal creature "alienated from the life of God," "lost" and "perishing"—should not the very faithfulness which guarantees science mean that God will take extraordinary steps to meet man's extraordinary need? Of course it does, and it is very significant that biblical miracles are all associated more or less closely with man's redemption from the slavery of sin, from alienation, to renewed fellowship with his Maker. It is in this light especially that we can view such great miracles of redemption as the Exodus, the Virgin

Birth of Jesus Christ, and the Resurrection.

Thus we reach the conclusion that the validity of the scientific enterprise is enhanced rather than weakened by the Bible's teaching on miracles; both the regular order built upon by science, and the "supernatural" which is the anchor of faith, are expressions, in response to different needs of man, of the very same attributes of God: his faithfulness and love.

Questions

1. In your own words, define "miracle."
2. Explain the apparent conflict between miracles and the laws of nature.
3. What is the purpose of miracles? Why does God allow them to be performed?
4. What does it mean to say God is immanent? Transcendent? What do those attributes have to do with whether miracles are rational or not?
5. Do you think miracles happen today? Why or why not?

Why Should I Believe That Jesus Is Anything More Than a Good Man or a Great Teacher?

Jesus and Paul Bunyan

James Ayers

James Ayers and a friend are discussing who Jesus is. His friend says that the story of Jesus has grown through the centuries, much like the legend of Paul Bunyan. But Ayers reminds him that there are many differences. One of the greatest is the fact that the Gospel writers were eye-witnesses to Jesus' life and ministry. No one claims to have known Paul Bunyan, and Paul Bunyan stories were tall tales from the beginning.

"Jesus does strike me as an intriguing figure, "said my friend. "I'm sure he was an inspiring teacher; maybe even what we'd call a prophet. But I doubt he ever thought of himself as more than that. After all, he called himself the Son of Man, didn't he?"

"Well, yes, he often did," I admitted.

"OK. It seems to me that he did a good job at being human, especially in comparison with the rest of us who mostly don't do so well. And he was popular. So his followers, probably some in the first century, then more as time went on, began to talk about him as more than merely human, and eventually to call him 'Son of God' and so on."

"It sounds like you're saying that the disciples and the early church made up stories about Jesus, stories that they knew weren't true. It always puzzles me when people suggest this, though. I can't understand why the disciples would do it. Why believe in someone when you yourself know that you invented the stories about him? If you don't have enough reason to believe in him, why bother to make up stories?"

"I'd guess it wasn't quite that deliberate," he replied. "Instead, I imagine it happened kind of like the Paul Bunyan stories. We could probably find a real lumberjack named Paul Bunyan behind the legends, if we knew where to look: a big, strapping lad who worked hard and impressed people with his strength and perseverance. But over the years the stories about him grew: he could clear hundred-acre woodlots in an afternoon, he combed his beard with a pine tree. Obviously those parts aren't true. Sure, they're part of the story, but everyone is supposed to realize that it isn't something that actually happened. Well, why can't we apply the same principle to the New Testament? We ought to recognize some of the material as augmentations. It's understandable that the story should grow that way; but we shouldn't take it seriously when it does."

"So while there must have been something impressive about Jesus' life and teaching, the story has been blown out of proportion by his followers later on?" I asked.

"That's right."

"In other words, the first followers of Jesus knew him as he really was, a skilled rabbi who set their hearts on fire. They shared their recollections about him with each other, and with new people who joined up later. After some time had gone by, say 10 or 15 years, people's memories weren't quite as clear, and some of them started to sneak in a miracle story every once in a while—maybe with a preamble that said, 'Now you weren't along on this trip, but I remember when Jesus and Peter and I . . . ' Then those stories grew over the next 20 years or so. Most of the original 12 have died out by now, and the leaders of the second generation are beginning to say that Jesus was more than a miracle worker or a prophet: he's the Messiah, the great leader our nation looked for and missed out on. Except for our own group, that is; we didn't miss out. And finally, by the end of the first century, people were saying that he wasn't just the Messiah; he was the Son of God, who had come to earth from heaven to save his people. Is that it?"

"Yeah, basically" he said. "That sounds a little quick to me, though obviously no one knows about the exact dates. But probably that's how it happened."

"Let me suggest an alternative," I said. "I think the New Testament got written by people trying to understand someone who was different from anyone else they had ever met. That's one of the differences between the Jesus story and the Paul Bunyan story. No one claims to have known Paul Bunyan; the stories have come down to us as legends, or even as self-admitted tall tales. But the writers of the New Testament often claim they knew Jesus personally, lived with him, ate with him, talked at length with him. On the basis of this first-hand knowledge they tell us, 'This is what Jesus said and did. Here's what he told us about himself and about the purpose for which the Father sent him. No mere human being could have done such things or talked that way.'"

"I like my explanation better," he said.

"I expect that many people during the early centuries did, too. But sometimes you have to choose between the explanation you like and the one that fits the facts."

"The facts?" he queried. "Wait a minute. Haven't modern scholars shown that the way the church thought about Jesus did, indeed, develop or grow as time went on? Isn't that a fact?"

"Well, for several centuries after the writing of the New Testament, the people of the church kept on working to understand as best they could what the New Testament taught about Jesus. They wanted to be confident that they had gotten it right, and so they debated whether a given passage should be understood this way or that. Eventually, through this process of examination and debate, they achieved a consensus where they could say, 'This is what the Bible teaches.'

"But all that effort—the development, if you like—was to understand what the New Testament already said," I continued. "And there's no point in the history of the writing of the New Testament books when they don't say it. Paul identified Jesus as Messiah, Lord, and Son of God in his earliest letters—Galatians, Romans, I Thessalonians—all of them written in the early to-mid 50s, just a couple of decades after the crucifixion. That's not very long for the legends to grow. Mark said the same thing in the mid-to-late 60s. The Gospel of John sometimes uses a more vivid vocabulary, but if it was written at about the year 90, its conception of Jesus doesn't seem to have grown from theirs in the intervening quarter-century. What this all means is that in the very earliest documents of the church that we have, whenever they talk about Jesus, right from the start they talk about him in these exalted terms."

"That soon?" he asked.

"That soon. If the disciples shifted the picture of what Jesus was like, they didn't do it gradually: they did it suddenly and completely, within just a few years of his death. I suppose you could argue that the change happened because the apostles formed some kind of conspiracy, made up a bunch of stories that never happened, pretended that life comes from allegiance to this Christ-who-never-was, and then got themselves tortured and killed for the sake of what they knew was a lie. But the one thing you can't say is that there was a slow and gradual growth of legends about him. It just didn't happen that way."

Questions

1. Why does the author's friend think the story of Jesus grew like the legend of Paul Bunyan?
2. What facts about the Gospel narrative is he forgetting?
3. How important is it to you that the Bible contains eyewitness accounts of Jesus' life and ministry?

Are the Gospels Historically Reliable?

Michael Green

Michael Green answers the question of the reliability of the Gospels by pointing to various sources of evidence. Pagan writers, Jewish historians, and archaeology validate the Gospel narrative. In addition, the Gospels themselves and other New Testament writings confirm that what the Gospel writers say about Jesus is true.

Christianity is unashamedly an historical religion. That is why the reliability of the Gospels is an important matter.

The authenticity of the documents

Our first question must be, "Have we got the Gospels substantially as they were written, or have people tampered with them down the centuries?" Well, we are in a better position to assess the authenticity of the New Testament than of any other ancient document. The gap between the writing of Thucydides' History and the oldest manuscript we have of it is some 1500 years; in the case of Tacitus it is 800.

In striking contrast, we have manuscripts of all the Gospels written before AD 200, that is to say within a century of the originals. Indeed, we have a fragment of John's Gospel that experts date as early as AD 125. Thus the famous archaeologist, Professor Kenyon, could write,

> . . . the interval between the dates of the original composition and the earliest extant evidence becomes so small as to be negligible, and the last foundation for any doubt that the Scriptures have come down to us substantially as they were written has now been removed.

Non-Christian evidence

"Very well," you may say, "But what non-Christian evidence is there to back up what the Gospels say?" There are three answers to that: the evidence of the pagans, the Jews and of archaeology.

Pagan writers

You would not expect there to be much evidence in pagan writers about an obscure carpenter who lived in a backward province of the empire. But there is some. The Roman historian Tacitus, writing about AD 100, records Nero's persecution of Christians. "The name of Christian," he says, "comes to them from Christ, who was executed in the reign of Tiberius by the procurator, Pontius Pilate." (*Annals*, 15:44). Suetonius, writing about AD 120, knows that Jews were expelled from Rome as early as AD 49 through quarrelling over one Chrestus (*ie* Christus—they were pronounced the same).

The fullest account of Christian activities seen through Roman eyes comes to us in a long letter from Pliny the Younger, Governor of Bithynia about AD 110. He tells us of the spread of Christianity even in that far away province to such an extent that the pagan temples had to close down. He tells us that these Christians were not guilty of any wickedness, but used to gather every morning to sing a hymn to Christ as God, and that they refused to bow down to the Emperor's statue or to deny the name of Jesus (*Epistles*, 10:96).

Jewish writings

The references in the Jewish writings are, of course, hostile to Jesus. They tell us that Jesus practised magic, deceived the people, healed the sick, had disciples, added to the Law, and was executed. Thus the Jerusalem Talmud says: "On the Eve of Passover they hanged Yeshu of Nazareth." The Jewish historian Josephus, writing at the end of the first century, knows that Jesus was the brother of James, claimed to be the Messiah, worked miracles, was crucified under Pilate, and was reputed to have risen from the dead (see particularly *Antiquities*, 18:3:3).

It is interesting that all these Jewish sources admit that Jesus performed miracles; but they attributed them to demonic powers, and sorceries learned in Egypt. (Is this indirect confirmation of Matthew 2:13 ff?)

Archaeology

Archaeology can help a little, too. It has thrown light upon the census recorded in Luke 2. It has produced a fascinating Imperial edict, dated between AD 20 and 50, saying nobody must disturb the tombs of the dead. This was found in Nazareth, and looks very much like official reaction to the resurrection. Evidence of a Christian church (including the Lord's Prayer) was found in the Italian towns of Herculaeneum and Pompeii, overcome by the eruption of Mount Vesuvius in AD 79.

Recently Professor Sukenik, a Jewish archaeologist discovered this scribbled prayer on a Jerusalem ossuary (bone-casket): "Jesus, Jesus, let him arise." The date? *Before AD 50!* Think of the implication of those simple words—the deity of Christ, the truth of the resurrection, and so on. Thus the broad historical reliability of the main events recorded in the Gospels can be substantiated from non-Christian sources.

Internal evidence

But what of the Gospels themselves?

The great thing to remember is that they are an entirely new literary *genre*. Obviously they are not biographies of Jesus. What biography would fail to tell us any of the physical features of its hero, pass over thirty years of his life without mention, or concentrate half the book on his death? They are not histories, either; thus the evangelists are not much interested in the chronology of the events they record. They are the proclamation of good news about Jesus whom his disciples had come to believe was God's Saviour, sent for all men.

How far can we rely on them?

Professor C.H. Dodd has shown, in his *Apostolic Preaching and its Development*, that much the same pattern of preaching can be found in all the different and independent strands which go to make up the New Testament. There can be little doubt that it faithfully represents the original Christian preaching about Jesus. Some of what the evangelists record can be checked. Thus the existence of eye-witnesses in the sixties, when Mark's Gospel appeared, is some guarantee of the truthfulness of his record—otherwise it would have been discredited. Now Mark's Gospel, as any commentary will tell you, is not only one of the main sources of Matthew and Luke; it records the preaching of Peter. Thus it takes us back to the very earliest Christian message.

Again, had the Church "cooked up" the contents of the Gospels, we would have expected to find them putting into Jesus' mouth matters of burning interest to themselves. But on the contrary, we find that the concerns of the early Church (the Lordship of Jesus, the Holy Spirit, the Jew-Gentile split, the circumcision issue, and so on) are conspicuous by their absence. Again, why make Jesus speak in parables, if he did not? Nobody in the early Church used parables, but the evangelists knew well that Jesus did. Nobody in the early Church called Jesus "Son of Man," but they knew he had used this title of himself. Indeed, although the evangelists felt free to alter the setting of Jesus' sayings, they paid meticulous respect to the sayings themselves. This suggests that the words of Jesus were, from the earliest times, treated as sacrosanct by the Church.

But how about John? Surely that is late and unreliable?

In recent years that estimate has had to be radically altered. For one thing, the sort of language used by Jesus in John ("children of light," "doing the truth," etc.), so far from being, as was once thought, a mark of lateness, has now been discovered in the Dead Sea Scrolls, a hundred years or so before John's Gospel was written.

Furthermore, recent excavations have shown that John's Gospel is incredibly accurate, even where it seemed to be the reverse. Thus critics used to laugh at the Pool of Bethesda—there was no trace of it on the ground or in ancient literature.

But now the pool has been discovered, and the name too has turned up in one of the Dead Sea Scrolls! Again, John's statement that Jesus was tried at a place called Gabbatha, the "place of the pavement" (John 19:13), was disbelieved, and regarded as unhistorical embroidery. No one knew anything about such a pavement, until Père Vincent dug it up, some 20 feet below the surface of Jerusalem. It is 50 yards square, and was part of the Roman barracks of Antonia, destroyed in the fall of Jerusalem in AD 70 . . . and not seen again till 1934. That means that this information of John's Gospel comes from before AD 70; not so late and unreliable after all! Indeed, St. John's Gospel is now thought, by some leading modern scholars, to have been formed, even if not actually written, before AD 60.

There is no space to go further into this fascinating subject. If you want more, read Professor F.F. Bruce's book, *The New Testament Documents: Are they Reliable?* (IVP) or A.M. Hunter's *According to John* (SCM).

Questions

1. What three sources of non-Christian evidence support the authenticity of the Gospels?
2. Why were the Gospels not written as biographies of Jesus or histories of his ministry?
3. Is it important to you that the Gospels be historically reliable? Does it really make any difference? Why or why not?

If Christianity Is True, Why Is the Church Full of Hypocrites?

Cafeteria Talk

L. Fischer

L. Fischer and a friend, Sol, are discussing religion in an African university cafeteria. Sol has seen a lot of Christianity, and he isn't impressed. White missionaries and African Christians are hypocrites, he says, because they say one thing and do another. When he needed help the Christians turned away. The suggestion that Jesus actually lives inside a Christian is utterly laughable to Sol.

You know the sound of a cafeteria. The rattling of plates and silverware. The dull roar of a dozen conversations. But somehow you don't notice the sound when you're helping to make it.

Today Sol and I are talking in the cafeteria of an African university. Sol is black and African and very proud of it. I am a white American, trying to learn about Africa. We met in a class we have together.

He often brings up the subject of religion. He knows I'm a

Christian. "But it's a cultural thing," he says. "Christianity is a part of your culture, not mine. Christianity is not for Africa, and it's not for me."

So here we are again, talking about religion over a Coke.

Sol objects to what he has seen in Christianity in the past. Christian missionaries and white colonialists in general exploited his people, looking down on them with a superior attitude. Sol explains, "The missionaries told us, 'Your way of life is inferior to ours. The way you dress is inferior. Your color is inferior. Your language is inferior.' They even advised us to discard our African names. They said, 'Change your names to the names of Bible characters or great Christians from Europe or America. Turn to God, and you will be like us.'

"But they are hypocrites," Sol continues—"missionaries and African Christians alike. What they say and what they do are two different things. They say we should live morally. But *they* don't. They say Christians should love each other. But they don't love, and they don't care. And when I needed help, they wouldn't help me. I came to the city to go to school. I had no income, no place to stay, no friends. I went to the Christians and they turned me away."

Sol's experiences were real. I had heard stories like his before. But I wish he knew some of the other Christians I have met in Africa.

I wish Sol knew people like Audu, the young professional man who read the New Testament, was impressed by its emphasis on love, and decided to become a Christian. Audu knew he might be killed for rejecting the religion of his family. He was afraid to go back home. But he did return to his people because he wanted to share God's love with them.

By now Sol and I have finished our Cokes, but we continue to talk. He asks me questions, and I ask him questions. And in the discussion I mention that a Christian has Christ in him and. . . .

Sol interrupts. His voice is deliberate and challenging, "Do you really think Christ is in you?"

"Well" . . . (I wasn't expecting that.) "Well . . . yes."

And Sol leans back in his chair and laughs. Not just a little snicker, but a long, deep laugh, really letting it go.

Then I start laughing too. I guess it really does sound funny. I mean, here I am saying that *God*, the one who made the whole world and keeps it going, is in *me*. Me, sitting here on a chair in the cafeteria. Me, with my notebook lying on the table next to me.

I wonder if Sol can see Christ in me.

Questions

1. Why does Sol believe the white missionaries and African Christians were hypocrites? Do you think they may have been? Why or why not?
2. Are all missionaries like those Sol describes? Do you think missionaries today tend to be more or less like that? Do you know of examples?
3. Why does Sol laugh at the conclusion of the conversation? Would you have laughed, too? Why or why not?
4. Do you think others can see Christ living in you?

Two-Faced People

Tim Stafford

Tim Stafford is a writer who is not afraid to tackle tough questions in the Christian life. This selection is excerpted from the book Secrets of the Christian Life. *He says that hypocrites are "counterfeit Christians" who pretend to be Christians because they think knowing God is going to benefit them in some way. His response is to feel sadness for them. He also says that self-examination is important because in many ways he's not much better than they are.*

I shall call him Mr. Thomas. He seldom missed church. He always prayed longer than anyone else and was most concerned about the "spiritual" dimensions of any problem. Yet he had cheated his relatives out of the family business, was a snoop, a liar, and to top it all off, overweight. Though I haven't seen him in years, I would still find it hard to enjoy shaking hands with him. He exuded slime. When I hear the word *hypocrite* I think of him.

Hypocrites are an easy excuse. Ask someone why he doesn't go to church, for instance, and you are likely to hear, "Because the church is full of hypocrites."

That answer helps him avoid saying, "Because I don't want to get up Sunday mornings" or "Because I don't believe in God the way Christians do" or even "Because I like my life the way it is and don't want to get close to something that might make me change." Any of these three, and plenty of others, would be decent reasons.

But someone who says the church is full of hypocrites puts his questioner on the defensive and doesn't have to deal with the real issues. That is why I have heard this excuse so often. I have also heard many Christians stumble and hedge defensively when they hear it.

I overheard a non-Christian friend try a variation of it. When asked why he wasn't a Christian, he explained that he had been raised a Catholic. He described several things wrong with the nuns he had encountered: their uptightness, their severity, the mumbo-jumbo they pushed on him. He was hung-up with those nuns; that was why, he said, he wasn't a Christian.

The person asking the question then broke into a delightful laugh. "You mean," he asked incredulously, "that you're going to let a few little ladies in uniforms keep you from knowing God?"

Since I heard that, I have had an answer when someone tells me hypocrites keep him from becoming a Christian. I use the same incredulous response. "Are you trying to say that a few hypocrites are enough to keep you from meeting God personally?"

That helps deal with the excuse, leaving you free to talk about genuine issues. But aren't there times when hypocrites are a genuine issue? For most people they are just an excuse, but are they always? Even as a Christian I am bothered by the existence of hypocrites—people like Mr. Thomas. They raise troublesome questions. If Christianity is so wonderful, why aren't Christians more wonderful people?

Why is it you find liars in the same building where truth is exalted week after week? Why does the religion that praises honesty have phonies everywhere? It's as shocking as going into a presidential candidate's headquarters and finding that his workers plan to vote against him. The insincerity surrounding the candidate makes you doubt the candidate himself.

It is the real question, not the excuse, that I want to deal with here. Why are there hypocritical Christians, and what are we supposed to do with them?

A hypocrite might be called a counterfeit Christian, and that word sheds light. Why do people counterfeit something? Only because that something is valuable. No one counterfeits a traffic ticket. No one fakes a bad report card. Only the more valuable things are counterfeited: things like twenty-dollar bills.

People will pretend to be rich. They will fake being university professors or football players. They will not usually pretend to be child beaters.

More than anything, people pretend to know God intimately. Why? Because knowing God is such a valuable thing, they want people to think they do. In a way, the presence of hypocrites demonstrates how desirable real Christianity is.

A generation ago, people would join the church because that was what all decent people did. Today you don't lose respect if you don't go to church or claim to be a Christian. The only reason to be a hypocritical Christian is that you think knowing God is valuable.

I do not mean that hypocrites consciously calculate how to "counterfeit" Christianity. What is a hypocrite? He is someone trying to gain respect from every group he's in. Around Christians he acts spiritual, because that is what he thinks will make him admired. Around other circles he acts unspiritual, because that will win him admiration or power. He is a chameleon, colored by whatever environment he's in. Not having enough character to be himself, he is forced to try to live up to a set of contradictory standards.

Of course, he gains only misery. He doesn't fool many people for long. Christians are not the only ones disgusted by a hypocrite; even those who live unspiritually all the time look down on someone who tries to have it both ways.

So when I recognize a hypocrite, I have learned that the proper attitude is sadness. I am seeing a person who doesn't know who he really is. He is too weak to be consistent, and he is probably miserable.

It is one thing to know sadness is the proper attitude, and another to practice it. I think of Mr. Thomas again. I have a hard enough time loving family and friends. How am I to love this man, so repulsively false?

The only way is to see deeper into him: to see the misery in his soul, and also to see somehow the real person buried under piles of lies and fears. Somewhere inside must be the person God made.

But how can I ignore all the obvious faults in a Mr. Thomas? How can I discover the person God meant him to be if he can't discover it himself? I find that I understand someone like him only when I examine my own life carefully. When I look deeply into my own soul I discover that I am not much better than Mr. Thomas.

A hypocrite is someone who says he believes one thing but lives another. By that standard I am a hypocrite, and so are you. In fact, there is no one who claims to be a Christian who is not in one sense a hypocrite. Did not Jesus tell us, "You shall love the Lord your God with all your mind, soul and strength, and your neighbor as yourself"? And don't we agree that these words are the standard for life? But none of us lives up to those words. The greatest difference between me and Mr. Thomas is not whether or not I live up to my beliefs; on that score I am a failure too. The difference is in the attitude toward that failure.

Jesus once told a story about two men who prayed. The first man, a hypocritical religious leader, thanked God for the moral character he lived, which was considerably above the norm. The other man, a notorious crook, was so ashamed of himself he could barely speak to God. He did not thank God for anything. All he asked for was mercy. Jesus commented that the second man, not the first, was pleasing to God.

The man was not pleasing because he had sinned less, but because of his humble attitude. He knew his faults, and he didn't try to hide them.

Questions

1. What is a hypocrite? Why are some people hypocrites? Are they generally happy people?
2. What is the difference between a hypocrite and a searching, growing believer?

3. Jesus' story of the two men who prayed in the temple (Luke 18:9-14) places hypocrisy in focus. What was the difference between the two men? What does Jesus' parable teach us?

Nice People or New Men

C.S. Lewis

C.S. Lewis is one of the most widely read evangelical authors of the twentieth century. This selection is excerpted from his popular book Mere Christianity. *Lewis addresses this question: "If Christianity is true why aren't all Christians obviously nicer than non-Christians?" The world is a complex place and every individual has a different temperament, but all people, both "nasty" and "nice" people, are in need of God's redemption. That is the reason Jesus Christ came to this earth—to make new people, not just to improve the old ones.*

He meant what He said. Those who put themselves in His hands will become perfect, as He is perfect—perfect in love, wisdom, joy, beauty, and immortality. The change will not be completed in this life, for death is an important part of the treatment. How far the change will have gone before death in any particular Christian is uncertain.

I think this is the right moment to consider a question which is often asked: If Christianity is true why are not all Christians obviously nicer than all non-Christians? What lies behind that question is partly something very reasonable and partly something that is not reasonable at all. The reasonable part is this. If conversion to Christianity makes no improvement in a man's outward actions—if he continues to be just as snobbish or spiteful or envious or ambitious as he was before—then I think we must suspect that his "conversion" was largely imaginary; and after one's original conversion, every time one thinks one has made an advance, that is the test to apply. Fine feelings, new insights, greater interest in "religion" mean nothing unless they make our actual behaviour better; just as in an illness "feeling better" is not much good if the thermometer shows that your temperature is still going up. In that sense the outer world is quite right to judge Christianity by its results. Christ told us to judge by results. A tree is known by its fruit; or, as we say, the proof of the pudding is in the eating. When we Christians behave badly, or fail to behave well, we are making Christianity unbelievable to the outside world. The wartime posters told us that Careless Talk costs Lives. It is equally true that Careless Lives cost Talk. Our careless lives set the outer world talking; and we give them grounds for talking in a way that throws doubt on the truth of Christianity itself.

But there is another way of demanding results in which the outer world may be quite illogical. They may demand not merely that each man's life should improve if he becomes a Christian: they may also demand before they believe in Christianity that they should see the whole world neatly divided into two camps—Christian and non-Christian—and that all the people in the first camp at any given moment should be obviously nicer than all the people in the second. This is unreasonable on several grounds.

(1) In the first place the situation in the actual world is much more complicated than that. The world does not consist of 100 per cent Christians and 100 per cent non-Christians. There are people (a great many of them) who are slowly ceasing to be Christians but who still call themselves by that name: some of them are clergymen. There are other people who are slowly becoming Christians though they do not yet call themselves so. There are people who do not accept the full Christian doctrine about Christ but who are so strongly attracted by Him that they are His in a much deeper sense than they themselves understand. There are people in other religions who are being led by God's secret influence to concentrate on those parts of their religion which are in agreement with Christianity, and who thus belong to Christ without knowing it. For example, a Buddhist of good will may be led to concentrate more and more on the Buddhist teaching about mercy and to

leave in the background (though he might still say he believed) the Buddhist teaching on certain other points. Many of the good Pagans long before Christ's birth may have been in this position. And always, of course, there are a great many people who are just confused in mind and have a lot of inconsistent beliefs all jumbled up together. Consequently, it is not much use trying to make judgments about Christians and non-Christians in the mass. It is some use comparing cats and dogs, or even men and women, in the mass, because there one knows definitely which is which. Also, an animal does not turn (either slowly or suddenly) from a dog into a cat. But when we are comparing Christians in general with non-Christians in general, we are usually not thinking about real people whom we know at all, but only about two vague ideas which we have got from novels and newspapers. If you want to compare the bad Christian and the good Atheist, you must think about two real specimens whom you have actually met. Unless we come down to brass tacks in that way, we shall only be wasting time.

(2) Suppose we have come down to brass tacks and are now talking not about an imaginary Christian and an imaginary non-Christian, but about two real people in our own neighbourhood. Even then we must be careful to ask the right question. If Christianity is true then it ought to follow (a) That any Christian will be nicer than the same person would be if he were not a Christian. (b) That any man who becomes a Christian will be nicer than he was before. . . . Christian Miss Bates may have an unkinder tongue than unbelieving Dick Firkin. That, by itself, does not tell us whether Christianity works. The question is what Miss Bates's tongue would be like if she were not a Christian and what Dick's would be like if he became one. Miss Bates and Dick, as a result of natural causes and early upbringing, have certain temperaments: Christianity professes to put both temperaments under new management if they will allow it to do so. What you have a right to ask is whether that management, if allowed to take over, improves the concern. Everyone knows that what is being managed in Dick Firkin's case is much "nicer" than what is being managed

in Miss Bates's. That is not the point. To judge the management of a factory, you must consider not only the output but the plant. Considering the plant at Factory A it may be a wonder that it turns out anything at all; considering the first-class outfit at Factory B its output, though high, may be a great deal lower than it ought to be. No doubt the good manager at Factory A is going to put in new machinery as soon as he can, but that takes time. In the meantime low output does not prove that he is a failure.

(3) And now, let us go a little deeper. The manager is going to put in new machinery: before Christ has finished with Miss Bates, she is going to be very "nice" indeed. But if we left it at that, it would sound as though Christ's only aim was to pull Miss Bates up to the same level on which Dick had been all along. We have been talking, in fact, as if Dick were all right; as if Christianity was something nasty people needed and nice ones could afford to do without; and as if niceness was all that God demanded. But this would be a fatal mistake. The truth is that in God's eyes Dick Firkin needs "saving" every bit as much as Miss Bates. In one sense (I will explain what sense in a moment) niceness hardly comes into the question.

You cannot expect God to look at Dick's placid temper and friendly disposition exactly as we do. They result from natural causes which God Himself creates. Being merely temperamental, they will all disappear if Dick's digestion alters. The niceness, in fact, is God's gift to Dick, not Dick's gift to God. In the same way, God has allowed natural causes, working in a world spoiled by centuries of sin, to produce in Miss Bates the narrow mind and jangled nerves which account for most of her nastiness. He intends, in His own good time, to set that part of her right. But that is not, for God, the critical part of the business. It presents no difficulties. It is not what He is anxious about. What He is watching and waiting and working for is something that is not easy even for God, because, from the nature of the case, even He cannot produce it by a mere act of power. He is waiting and watching for it both in Miss Bates and in Dick Firkin. It is something they can freely give Him. Will they, or will they not, turn to Him and thus fulfill the only purpose for which they were created? Their free will is trembling inside them like the needle of a compass. But this is a needle that can choose. It *can* point to its true North; but it need not. Will the needle swing round, and settle, and point to God?

He can help it to do so. He cannot force it. He cannot, so to speak, put out His own hand and pull it into the right position, for then it would not be free will any more. Will it point North? That is the question on which all hangs. Will Miss Bates and Dick offer their natures to God? The question whether the natures they offer or withhold are, at that moment, nice or nasty ones, is of secondary importance. God can see to that part of the problem.

Do not misunderstand me. Of course God regards a nasty nature as a bad and deplorable thing. And, of course, He regards a nice nature as a good thing—good like bread, or sunshine, or water. But these are the good things which He gives and we receive. He created Dick's sound nerves and good digestion, and there is plenty more where they came from. It costs God nothing, so far as we know, to create nice things: but to convert rebellious wills cost Him crucifixion. And because they are wills they can—in nice people just as much as in nasty ones— refuse His request. And then, because that niceness in Dick was merely part of nature, it will all go to pieces in the end. Nature herself will all pass away. Natural causes come together in Dick to make a pleasant psychological pattern, just as they come together in a sunset to make a pleasant pattern of colours. Presently (for that is how nature works) they will fall apart again and the pattern in both cases will disappear. Dick has had the chance to turn (or rather, to allow God to turn) that momentary pattern into the beauty of an eternal spirit: and he has not taken it.

There is a paradox here. As long as Dick does not turn to God, he thinks his niceness is his own, and just as long as he thinks that, it is not his own. It is when Dick realises that his niceness is not his own but a gift from God, and when he offers it back to God—it is just then that it begins to be really his own. For now Dick is beginning to take a share in his own creation. The only things we can keep are the things we freely give to God. What we try to keep for ourselves is just what we are sure to lose.

We must, therefore, not be surprised if we find among the Christians some people who are still nasty. There is even, when you come to think it over, a reason why nasty people might be expected to turn to Christ in greater numbers than nice ones. That was what people objected to about Christ during his life on earth: He seemed to attract "such awful people." That is what people still object to, and always will. Do you not see why? Christ said, "Blessed are the poor" and "How hard it is for the rich to enter the Kingdom," and no doubt He primarily meant the economically rich and economically poor. But do not His words also apply to another kind of riches and poverty? One of the dangers of having a lot of money is that you may be quite satisfied with the kinds of happiness money can give and so fail to realise your need for God. If everything seems to come simply by signing checks, you may forget that you are at every moment totally dependent on God. Now quite plainly, natural gifts carry with them a similar danger. If you have sound nerves and intelligence and health and popularity and a good upbringing, you are likely to be quite satisfied with your character as it is. "Why drag God into it?" you may ask. A certain level of good conduct comes fairly easily to you. You are not one of those wretched creatures who are always being tripped up by sex, or dipsomania, or nervousness, or bad temper. Everyone says you are a nice chap and (between ourselves) you agree with them. You are quite likely to believe that all this niceness is your own doing: and you may easily not feel the need for any better kind of goodness. Often people who have all these natural kinds of goodness cannot be brought to recognise their need for Christ at all until, one day, the natural goodness lets them down and their self-satisfaction is shattered. In other words, it is hard for those who are "rich" in this sense to enter the Kingdom.

It is very different for the nasty people—the little, low, timid, warped, thin-blooded, lonely people, or the passionate, sensual, unbalanced people. If they make any attempt at goodness at all, they learn, in double quick time, that they need help. It is Christ or nothing for them. It is taking up the cross and following—or else despair. They are the lost sheep; He came specially to find them. They are (in one very real and terrible sense) the "poor": He blessed them. They are the "awful set" he goes about with—and of course the Pharisees say still, as they said from the first, "If there were anything in Christianity those people would not be Christians."

There is either a warning or an encouragement here for every one of us. If you are a nice person—if virtue comes easily to you—beware! Much is expected from those to whom much is given. If you mistake for your own merits what are really God's gifts to you through nature, and if you are contented with simply being nice, you are still a rebel: and all those gifts will only make your fall more terrible, your corruption more complicated, your bad example more disastrous. The Devil was an archangel once; his natural gifts were as far above yours as yours are above those of a chimpanzee.

But if you are a poor creature—poisoned by a wretched up-bringing in some house full of vulgar jealousies and senseless quarrels—saddled, by no choice of your own, with some loathsome sexual perversion—nagged day in and day out by an inferiority complex that makes you snap at your best friends—do not despair. He knows all about it. You are one of the poor whom He blessed. He knows what a wretched machine you are trying to drive. Keep on. Do what you can. One day (perhaps in another world, but perhaps far sooner than that) he will fling it on the scrap-heap and give you a new one. And then you may astonish us all—not least yourself: for you have learned your driving in a hard school. (Some of the last will be first and some of the first will be last.)

"Niceness"—wholesome, integrated personality—is an excellent thing. We must try by every medical, educational, economic, and political means in our power, to produce a world where as many people as possible grow up "nice"; just as we must try to produce a world where all have plenty to eat. But we must not suppose that even if we succeeded in making everyone nice we should have saved their souls. A world of nice people, content in their own niceness, looking no further, turned away from God, would be just as desperately in need of salvation as a miserable world—and might even be more difficult to save.

For mere improvement is not redemption, though redemption always improves people even here and now and will, in the end, improve them to a degree we cannot yet imagine. God became man to turn creatures into sons: not simply to produce better men of the old kind but to produce a new kind of man. It is not like teaching a horse to jump better and better but like turning a horse into a winged creature. Of course, once it has got its wings, it will soar over fences which could never have been jumped and thus beat the natural horse at its own game. But there may be a period, while the wings are just beginning to grow, when it cannot do so: and at that stage the lumps on the shoulders—no one could tell by looking at them that they are going to be wings—may even give it an awkward appearance.

Questions

1. Is "niceness" all that God demands of people? What else does God demand?
2. Why is it "harder" for God to change a person's inner nature than to change a person's personality traits? Why is it more important for God to change the inner nature?
3. Of what value is "niceness" in this world? In this next world?

How Is Christianity Relevant to My Life?

The Unimportance of Being Christian

Paul Blanshard

Paul Blanshard claims to be a pastor, but he does not believe that it is important for anyone to be a Christian. He believes that preachers and evangelists do not preach the gospel. The Bible is incomprehensible and irrelevant. Modern morality is not ultimately based on the Bible. And the Church is good only for the promotion of democratic values. For Blanshard, Christianity is totally irrelevant—and, he says, it should be for you, too.

Young Self—1917

I talked not long ago with one of America's greatest Jewish leaders as he sat by the fireside with his family. His was an ideal home full of enlightenment and love. It was what we have learned to call a "Christian home." As we talked together of the problems of labor and social reform that confront us, I realized the true nobility and unselfishness of the man. Then the thought came to me, "How ridiculous it would seem for me to say that he was damned for his unbelief while I was saved by my Christianity." He had more of love and patience and idealism than I would ever have. He could convert me to Judaism sooner than I could win him to Christianity.

But I did not try to convert him to Christianity because I realized the unimportance of being Christian.

What I felt has been tacitly agreed upon by most Christians for a long time. Proselytizing for the Christian religion has become a lost art. I mean real proselytizing. When young men and women who have been surrounded by church influences all their lives finally reach the age of decision, their entrance into organized Christianity is as automatic and inevitable as their entrance into society. In fact it is little else but an entrance into moral society under the careful guidance of anxious parents. Put the same kind of children with the same kind of parents into Arabia and the apples would fall as readily into Mohammedan baskets.

When Billy Sunday preaching in a Christian nation after Christianity has been on trial for nearly two thousand years succeeds in winning several thousand converts to Christianity he is hailed as a remarkable teacher. He is a remarkable teacher. His success stands out in striking contrast to the failure of almost every other evangelist who has had the courage to preach Christianity in all its nakedness.

It requires no special investigation to discover that most people in America are genuinely indifferent to all that conversion implies. They are quite heedless of the preachers' solemn question, "Where will you spend eternity?" They do not know where they will spend eternity and they are quite certain that Christianity will not enlighten them in the matter. In the South and especially among the foreign workingmen who operate many of our greatest industries, hundreds are buried without funerals, utterly scornful even in their grief of the churches' teaching concerning life and death.

In opposition to this widespread indifference there are two classes of preachers who are successful in their proselytizing, modern and genial pastors who never preach Christianity, and the vaudeville evangelists who by their magnetic power shock people out of their normal littleness.

I belong to the first class. I have converted many people to my own conceptions of morality and religion with the help of biblical phrases and the authority which the church has given me, but I have never converted any one to the religion of Jesus Christ. For a long time I thought that I was a Christian evangelist. Now I know that there are very few Christian evangelists, and that the astute businessmen and special pleaders who fill our city pulpits are converting men not to Christianity but to certain moral standards of optimism, honesty, self-confidence and ambition that will guarantee their success in the present social system. If I, as a city pastor, should suddenly declare that unless my congregation abandoned their earthly work, took no thought for the morrow, trusted in God so much that the food supply should be obtained by prayer to the Father who promised through his Son that everyone who asked should receive, I would instantly be asked to resign.

Men would say that I was preaching insanity. The tragedy is that they would be right, and I would be Christian.

But the professional evangelists who are attempting to defend Christianity are a far more interesting study than the sensible city pastors. They are the true successors of St. Paul, earnest, enthusiastic, and successful, because they have reduced religion to a compact formula which even the most ignorant cannot mistake. How delightfully simple this formula is! Believe in the Lord Jesus Christ and thou shalt be saved. For the rest, be good!

The character of these evangelists betrays them. Even the laity is beginning to be suspicious of that character. I have met many evangelists and heard many more give forth the sound and fury of gospel heat, and I have never yet discovered an effective evangelist who had a good education coupled with sane and careful judgment. The foremost representatives of proselytizing Christianity are emotional calliopes who play upon the ignorance and emotional hunger of their audiences.

Some of them are sincere with the sincerity created by personal power and exciting success—it is hard for successful men to disbelieve in themselves and their mission. Some of them are sincere with the sincerity of unadulterated ignorance. Many of them are emotionally and morally rotten, afraid to face the simplest doubt with candid analysis.

The character of the revivalists throws suspicion upon the value of their message. It is not the falsehood of that message which impresses the observer so much as the unimportance of it. That unimportance is due at least partially to the remoteness of the message of the Bible.

The Bible is not only incomprehensible to the average man: It is incomprehensible to most scholars. This is not because of any unusual depth of reasoning but because it is the work of contradictory, untrained minds, speaking a language which we do not completely understand, and setting forth a view of life which we can appreciate only by the systematic stretching of a trained imagination. We cannot understand the Bible unless we can "put ourselves back" into Palestine and catch a glimpse of the world as it appeared to Jewish prophets and priests. And when, after years of special training, the scholar succeeds in realizing something of the real biblical viewpoint, he sees how little vitality there is in the message which ancient Jewish sages bring to us. . . .

When a careful study is made of the people to whom the Bible is preeminently important, it will be found in almost every case that they are either professionals who must use the Bible in the development of their careers or ignorant people whose range of reading is so limited that the narratives and exhortations of the Bible are interesting. Because the Bible was the only serious and vital literature in so many thousands of the homes of our grandfathers it became for them a genuinely sacred book. It contained the only philosophy and poetry they ever read. In a life of endless monotony and commonplaceness, it was the only thing that demanded their reverence.

But with expanding knowledge, the Bible is gradually taking its more natural place with the other dust-covered articles on the parlor table or the bottom shelf of the family bookcase. Nehemiah, Jehoshphat, and their kind are described in the Sunday school and then promptly forgotten. In the life of America the Bible has already become an unimportant symbol, like a literary rosary, to be purchased and occasionally thumbed through but seldom to be read.

There is another and much more significant indication of the unimportance of Christianity in our time. The moral ideas of the race when frankly examined show practically no dependence upon the maintenance of Christianity.

Even in the questions of personal morals we do not follow distinctively Christian standards. The reason is that there are no Christian standards that can be effectively used in solving our ordinary moral problems.

If I consult the teachings of Jesus in regard to wine-drinking, I cannot discover whether I should be a total abstainer or not. Jesus did not know anything about American saloons. If I am anxious to know whether a divorced person can be married again, I find that the teachings of Jesus are ambiguous. Jesus was never married and he knew nothing of syphilis, low wages for working girls or the feminist movement. If I hesitate before entering the army and ask myself, "Is it possible for a Christian to be a soldier?" I find that Jesus can readily be made into a Quaker pacifist or a terrible fighter for all just causes. If I turn to the teachings of Jesus to find standards for honesty while earning a living, I find nothing beyond vague moral generalizations. Jesus knew nothing of modern trusts, cutthroat competition and business honesty.

In the absence of definite Christian standards of morality, Christianity becomes merely a label for the particular moral system we want to endorse. No one can tell the world what Christianity really is, so everybody's religious business becomes nobody's religious business. What Christianity really is becomes unimportant. What the moral habits of the race are become all-important.

The thing we call Christianity will live for many centuries because it has succeeded in gathering unto itself the greatest

moral qualities of the race and in using those qualities to bol-
ster up an antiquated analysis of life and an institution that
still dominates our moral horizon. So it has become a mixture
of the most practical and noble truths with the most ridiculous
deceptions. In the same breath we are asked to believe that we
should love our neighbors, and that a certain fish swallowed
Jonah and kept him in the submarine stateroom for three days.
We are asked to accept the gospel of peace, and to believe that
peace can come only through the belief by all humanity that
God became completely incarnate in a certain Jewish prophet
who lived many centuries ago.

As we confront this queer, impossible mixture, we cannot
feel that it is important for any man to be a Christian. Obviously, the one important task of our time is to work for that
society based upon more equal opportunity which is the ideal
of all men whose faces "are turned toward the light." When
we have glimpsed this larger vision, we cannot help but recognize the real irrelevancy of Christian proselytizing.

But the unimportance of being Christian does not include
the unimportance of having churches. Quite apart from its
function as an agent for the Christian Gospel the church is an
organization of human beings met together for the purpose of
reflection, service, and fellowship. In the vast arid desert of
our unorganized life any church that brings the people together in fellowship is doing much for human life.

The old village tavern taught the people of the countryside
what they knew of gossip, manners and politics. That social
function was connected with the flowing bowl, but even the
temperance reformer must recognize that the old tavern sup-
plied a fundamental social need of the community. It brought
men from loneliness into comradeship at a time when no other
institution served that purpose. It taught men to know one
another and to know themselves. It laid the basis of democracy.

So the church is helping the cause of democracy by bringing men under one roof who think and talk together of the
common moral problems of the race. It is often dominated by
class interests and unspeakably hypocritical, but to the man

who observes *all*, life *is* dominated by class interests and unspeakably hypocritical. The church is no worse and probably a little better than most of our institutions. It is the only moral forum in thousands of communities; it is the most natural meeting-ground for those who are striving to do good. Until we have a better forum for the development of a people's philosophy and ethics, blessed be the church!

It is upon this rock that the enemy of the church most often flounders. He denounces the church and praises what he calls "real Christianity." If he had studied the situation, his attitude would be just the reverse.

I have become an enemy of the Christian church but not an enemy of the church. I believe in the church but deny Christianity. I believe in the church not because of what it is today but because of the possibilities of a great temple of religious aspiration and moral reflection in the midst of a community whose thoughts are bent on petty things.

Ostensibly the church was built on Christianity, but it is now built upon something far more profound. Its real foundation is the craving for fellowship and the universal desire of men to know the secrets of life. The real basis of the public school is not White's *Arithmetic* or any other particular textbook, but the desire of the people for general learning.

Likewise the church. Eject Christianity (as it has already been partially ejected), substitute the religion and morals that each community works out for itself and you have a church more powerful than ever. The demand for such an institution will never die. Humanity must always go to church to learn more of the great mysteries of life, death and conduct. When the unimportance of Christianity and the importance of the churches have been realized, then the church will reshape itself to meet the needs of a wiser and a frankly un-Christian world.

Questions

1. Blanshard says that he belongs to the class of "successful, modern, genial pastors who never preach Christianity." What kind of gospel do you think Blanshard preaches? Does he seem happy or content?
2. What is "the one important task of our time," according to Blanshard? On what is it based?
3. How does Blanshard describe the role and function of the Church?
4. What is Blanshard's view of the Bible? Why should it be relegated to "the bottom shelf of the family bookcase"? What should take its place?
5. Blanshard says that he cannot feel that it is important for anyone to be a Christian. How do you respond and why?

Christ Is Relevant Today

Paul Little

Paul Little's book How to Give Away Your Faith *has helped thousands of young Christians gain the confidence they need to witness for Christ. In this selection Little tells how Jesus Christ meets the specific personal needs of many people today.*

The question uppermost in the minds of people today is not, Is Christianity true? They have a more practical question on their minds: Is it relevant? Student reaction is often: "So I believe what you've said about Jesus Christ—so what? What's it got to do with modern life? What's it got to do with me?" If we want to speak of Jesus Christ today, we need to have in the forefront of our minds how he is personally relevant to us. From there we can consider how to relate the events that took place two thousand years ago to life in the twentieth century.

This is a day when conversations about spiritual realities are part of everyday social interchange. The day of the taboo on "religion and politics" is gone. And the need for such discussion couldn't be greater. Shortly before his death, the late Dr. Karl Compton of Massachusetts Institute of Technology warned that humankind faces annihilation unless the human race soon achieves moral and spiritual advances equivalent to its technological advances.

Life magazine, in reporting the Nobel prize winners in physics several years ago, pointed out that the tremendously rapid advances in scientific understanding have been mere arithmetic gains in comparison to the geometric gains of ignorance. Each additional discovery multiplies our realization of how much we do not know and cannot control. It also enables us to manipulate extensive new areas for ill as well as for good. For instance, nuclear energy can be used to destroy cities or cancer. Genetic engineering that is designed to aid us can backfire into unthinkable disasters. In spite of the fact that many attempt to keep morality separate from science, ethical and metaphysical issues are more openly investigated and to the point today than ever before.

Inner Emptiness

Many thoughtful people now realize that they cannot subsist on a diet of platitudes. How is the living Christ relevant to them? In considering present and eternal human needs, we find that the relevance of Jesus Christ to twentieth-century people is disclosed by his own words. The "I am" designations recorded in the Gospel of John give us a clue as we see their relationship to modern people and their needs.

One basic need is for a filling of the spiritual vacuum, an answer to the inner emptiness that plagues many lives today. People often immerse themselves, in fact, lose themselves, in all kinds of activity and external stimulation. Remove that external stimulation, get them alone with their thoughts, and they're bored, anxious or miserable. They feel the aching void within, and they can't escape it. They realize their lack of inner resources for the tests of life; all their props are external. Nothing external can produce lasting satisfaction. Satisfaction that lasts must come from what is inside us.

The Lord Jesus Christ says in John 6:35, "I am the bread of life. He who comes to me will never go hungry, and he who believes in me will never be thirsty."

A tremendous thing happens when we become personally related to Jesus Christ as a living person. He enters our inner beings and fills our spiritual vacuums as only he can. Because he is inside us through the indwelling presence of the Holy Spirit, we can have ultimate satisfaction. Augustine and many others throughout the centuries have echoed this discovery: "Thou hast made us for Thyself, O God, and our hearts are restless till they find their rest in Thee." God constructed us this way—creatures dependent on our Creator for completion and fulfillment. We can function as our Maker intended only when he is occupying the very center of our lives.

Being released from dependence on external things for stimulation and pleasure in life is like sitting down to a sirloin steak after months of eating potato peelings. When we stop depending on outward and material things, we don't have to stop enjoying them. We can enjoy a concert, for instance, or the beauty of a sunset, to the glory of God. But we no longer depend on these things for our satisfaction in life. Like our Lord, we have food to eat which others do not, namely, doing the will of our Father in heaven (John 4:32). We draw from the resources that we have within us through the Lord Jesus Christ. We enjoy but do not depend on externals.

Jesus Christ is "the thing" many people are longing to get hold of. He is the one who will fill their aching void and free them from their false dependencies.

Purposelessness

Another major area of need is the aimlessness, the purposelessness that characterizes our age. I see it repeatedly in the student world. Many come up to me after a discussion and say, "You described me exactly. I don't know what I'm doing here in the university. I don't know why I'm eating three meals a day, studying architecture (physics, or whatever). I'm here because my folks are paying the bill, but I can't see what it's all about or what it's all leading to. I'm caught in a rat race of daily routines. It's hard to keep plugging away at the books when you can't see where you're going or why."

To this need the Lord Jesus Christ says, "I am the light of the world. Whoever follows me will never walk in darkness, but will have the light of life" (John 8:12).

When we follow the Lord we discover a purpose and direction for our lives, because we are living in the light of God himself and of his will for us. We are no longer fumbling in the darkness of confusion. Have you ever groped about in a dark room trying to find the light switch? You brush against something. Then you feel something else trail across your face. You jump three feet and knock over a waste basket. Your heart skips a beat. You know this uncertain, insecure feeling. At last you find the light switch, turn it on and orient yourself. Immediately you're secure. You know exactly how to proceed. Our experience is similar when we come to know the Lord Jesus Christ. He leads us out of our confusion and uncertainty into his light. We see our lives in the context of God's will and purpose for history. That vision bestows significance, meaning and purpose.

Most of God's will is already revealed for us in Scripture. When we are obeying the will of God as we know it, he will make more of the details of his will clear to us. When we have told him we're ready to accept his will whatever it may be, he gradually discloses to us additional details about where we should be and what we should do. As a scroll unwinds, so he shows to us, his children, his divine purposes.

These details, which mean so much to us individually, are in one sense quite incidental to the basic purpose of God. He is calling out for himself a people from every tribe and tongue and nation, a people who will individually manifest the likeness of Christ. This is what God is doing in history. When he brings history to its conclusion, you and I will have the privilege of being part of God's eternal work.

Our lives have significance, meaning and purpose not only for this life but for eternity. Think of it! Many people have some purpose in life at this moment. But most of these purposes are short-lived. They won't give ultimate satisfaction; they don't mean a thing in terms of eternity. To have ultimate meaning our lives must count not only for time, but also for eternity. We see so many people today who don't know what life is all about; they're groping around in darkness without Christ. They're as aimless as a ship without a rudder. If we relate the Lord Jesus Christ to them as the one who fulfills our need for direction and makes life purposeful, they may be attracted to him and let him meet their needs.

Fear of Death

A third need that the Lord Jesus Christ can meet is our

need for an antidote to the fear of death. When we're young, death tends to be academic. We don't expect to die soon, so we don't give the possibility much thought. But death can rapidly become a prime consideration.

In this nuclear age, an amazing number of young people have begun to think hard about death. They're keenly aware that we live on the brink of destruction. One push of a button and everything could be gone. In a 1984 national opinion poll, George Gallup asked which problem facing the United States was felt to be the most serious. The overwhelming majority of those polled listed the threat of annihilation by nuclear war as our primary threat in this decade as well as in the year 2000. While not always in the forefront of our thinking, the destructiveness of the bomb lurks beneath the surface. It is not only that we possess the power to destroy civilization but any one of our enemies in the "nuclear club" also has that capability.

Frantically we try to avoid other forms of imminent death by lessening alcohol consumption, avoiding cholesterol and not smoking. *The New York Times* reported that with these restrictions a forty-five-year-old man can live about eleven years longer, a forty-five-year-old woman could add an extra seven years to her life. Then around the corner comes the as-yet-uncontrollable killer AIDS. Young people fear contamination by person-to-person contact. Older people fear infection through illnesses that require blood transfusions. The slow-moving train of death cannot be avoided, nor can it be faced.

To this kind of fearful world the Lord Jesus Christ speaks with power about death. In John 11:25-26, he says, "I am the resurrection and the life. He who believes in me will live, even though he dies; and whoever lives and believes in me will never die." As we come to know him in personal experience, Jesus Christ delivers us from the fear of death. Death ceases to be an unknown. We know it is simply the servant that ushers us into the presence of the living God whom we love. This knowledge enabled Paul to exult, "Where, O death, is your victory? Where, O death, is your sting?" (1 Corinthians 15:55).

Instead of fearing death, we anticipate the most dynamic experience we can ever have.

I hope none of us has succumbed to the naive impression that heavenly existence is sitting on Pink Cloud Number Nineteen and strumming a harp. Naturally, we'd all be terribly bored with heaven after the first week. Lest we fall for such silly thoughts, let's be assured that heaven will not be a boring place. We don't have all the details, because God hasn't chosen to give them to us; but from what he has told us we can conclude that heaven will be a dynamic, expanding, creative experience far beyond anything our finite minds can now comprehend. It will be the essence of joy and satisfaction and song. Even though we don't fully understand what heaven will be, we look forward to being forever with the Lord. So we can suggest to others that Jesus Christ himself is the solution to their present fears of death.

Until we ourselves face the prospect of death, however, we may not be sure experientially that Christ delivers us from this fear. It's wonderfully easy to say he does, as you relax with friends around a warm fire after a scrumptious meal. It's quite different to say it when you're actually facing death.

Situations such as impending surgery often bring individuals face to face with the fact of dying. When I underwent heart surgery at age twenty-four, I saw in the depths of my own experience Christ's power to conquer the fear of dying. This proof was a valuable by-product of the operation. Before, I'd always maintained that Christians don't fear death, but I couldn't speak from personal experience.

When they came in to inject the anesthetic the morning of the operation, I was keenly aware of my chances. This was before the days of life-support systems, and my surgeon had never done this particular procedure on an adult. I knew that in all likelihood I would come back from the operating room, and yet there was that other chance! A heart operation, you know, can be a complete success, but the patient may die because one of seventy-four other things has gone wrong.

Well, that morning as I was wheeled toward the operating

room, a joy and peace that had to come from outside of myself flooded my being. I'll never forget it. If I'd ever thought that peace in the face of death could be conjured up through the power of positive thinking, that idea was dispelled forever. I knew I didn't have it in me to face this crisis myself. Mortal fear had gripped the man across the hall who was going in for an appendectomy. If positive thinking could have done the trick, he could have talked himself out of his fear.

As for me, strains of *Messiah* pounded through my brain as I was rolled down the hall to the operating room. As the nurses dripped in the sodium pentothal, I could even joke with them about how long I would stay awake—I think I got to six before I lost consciousness. It was a wonderful experience for me to put this fact of reality to the test and prove it true. Because it is true, we can invite those seeking freedom from the fear of death to turn to the Lord Jesus Christ and find him a relevant solution to their fear.

Desire for Inner Peace

Another expression of need today is the longing for inner peace. A Christian doctor on the West Coast took an informal, three-year poll among his patients. He wanted to know what one wish each would make if assured that the wish would be granted. Peace of heart, mind and soul was the number one desire of eighty-seven per cent of his patients. The phenomenal sale of religious books in recent years also indicates this unmet need. People don't have inner peace, but they want it desperately. Deep down they realize that everything in this life—material possessions, power, prestige, fame—will turn to dust and ashes. They yearn for the lasting inner peace and contentment that transcends these passing things.

Again, our Lord Jesus himself supplies the answer to humanity's need. His promise in John 14:27 is more than sufficient: "Peace I leave with you; my peace I give you. I do not give to you as the world gives. Do not let your hearts be troubled."

His peace differs from the peace the world gives. The peace we find in the world may seem very real for the moment, but then it's gone. Jesus said he was not of the world (John 17:14). Therefore he can give a peace that transcends this world, a peace that is deepseated, permanent, eternal. This deep-seated peace of heart, mind and soul grows out of our personal relationship of faith and dependence on the Lord Jesus Christ. He only asks us to accept his invitation, "Come to me, all you who are weary and burdened, and I will give you rest" (Matthew 11:28). People would pay millions of dollars if rest could be bought with money. But it's not available that way. The Lord Jesus Christ only gives his peace to those who will receive it as a free gift.

Loneliness

Although we all have a basic need for love and security, loneliness is common today. A Harvard sociologist, David Riesman, emphasized this fact in his much-read book *The Lonely Crowd*. He points out that many people are only existing as shells in the midst of a crowd.

Our Lord has dynamically related himself to this particular need in saying, "I am the good shepherd. The good shepherd lays down his life for the sheep" (John 10:11).

A shepherd looks after and cares for the sheep. Our Lord cared so much that he gave his life for his sheep. He has further assured us with the words, "I am with you always, to the very end of the age" and "I will never leave you nor forsake you."

A student from Barnard College of Columbia University came to see my wife one afternoon while we were living in New York City. The woman was utterly alone and felt she couldn't trust anyone because of past experiences with family and friends. As Marie told her about some of the ways Jesus Christ would meet the needs in her life, she looked up with tears in her eyes and asked, "Do you mean that he would never leave me; that he would always love me if I committed my life to him?" My wife assured her that she meant just that, for the authority of our Lord's words and the proof of her own personal experience confirmed his faithfulness.

Has the presence of Jesus Christ ever dispelled your loneliness? Because I do a lot of traveling, I often find myself alone in Boondocks Junction, not knowing anyone. It's been wonderful at such times to claim the reality of the Lord's presence by faith and to recognize that I am never alone. It's tremendous knowing that we will never be alone because the Lord Jesus Christ is always with us. Sometimes when we imagine we're all alone, we're tempted to do things that we wouldn't do if we remembered Christ's abiding presence with us. But when we consciously recognize and live in the light of his presence, we have a negative deterrent from sin as well as a positive dynamic for life.

Lack of Self-Control

Many people face a problem of poor self-control: "I find myself doing things I never thought I'd indulge in. I vow I'm going to change, but I can't." When students open up about themselves, they almost always admit this problem. They've become involved in campus behavior that they would never have dreamed of back home. The maelstrom of social pressure sucks them in. Then, try as they will, they can't escape its grasp.

Our Lord speaks to this need by promising to give us life and power. In John 14:6 he says, "I am the way and the truth and the life."

As we rely on him, avoiding the temptations we would bring upon ourselves and trusting in his power to deliver us from the temptations that come unforeseen, he releases his power in our lives and transforms our lack of self-control into deliverance from the power of sin. This transforming power characterizes the lives of many who have come to know Jesus Christ. It is especially evident in people who have been converted out of pagan backgrounds into a drastically different pattern of life. Jesus Christ has broken their chains of lack of self-control and given them power that they know couldn't come from themselves. This is one of the most potent relevancies of Jesus Christ to twentieth-century humanity.

Our Thinking Needs Integration

In his words "I am the way and the truth and the life," our

Lord also speaks to another major need we have: integration in our thinking.

A University of Wisconsin senior approached a Christian faculty friend of mine with this problem: "I've completed my 144 credit hours, and in two weeks I'm going to graduate. But I feel like I'm leaving the university with a bagful of marbles in my hand. I don't see any relationships between the various courses I've studied. They don't seem to fit together. They're more like unrelated marbles in a bag." This fellow did not know him who is the Truth—the one who is absolute truth, from whom all truth stems, in whom all truth is interrelated and tied together. All kinds of things begin to fall into place in Jesus Christ as we come to see him as the one who ultimately is the only truth.

We have authority as Christians to speak of Jesus Christ because he is the Truth. We shouldn't communicate the gospel on mere pragmatic grounds, although the gospel is true pragmatically. Our approach does not present God as a cosmic bellboy who meets all our needs. We don't claim that Christianity is true because it works. No, Christianity works because it is true. Jesus Christ is the Truth.

Our Lord spoke with devastating authority when he said, "Heaven and earth will pass away, but my words will never pass away" (Mark 13:31). The message of Jesus Christ has a down-to-earth, pragmatic effect for one who trusts him. Though this is true, this is only one aspect of the message; it is not the message itself. Our primary message should be the revealed truth of God concerning our need for repentance and the redemption available through Jesus Christ. Then we can relate Jesus Christ to contemporary needs, showing the people around us that he can be relevant to them in personal experience. Our own personal experience of how Jesus Christ meets specific needs will help others to see how very relevant and reliable the promises of Jesus Christ are.

In this short chapter we certainly haven't covered all the needs of people in today's world, nor all the Lord's specific provisions for each of them. Neither are we pretending that once we receive Jesus Christ all our struggles are over. The Christian life is a warfare, and the two combatants, Jesus Christ and Satan, never call a draw. The profound, unchanging truth is that our Lord is the victor and is with us in the battle, and he makes all the difference in the world.

Questions

1. List the specific needs of people that Little describes. How does Jesus meet each of those needs?
2. Can a non-Christian have those needs met without Christ? Why or why not?

Are Christians Other-Worldly?

Gordon Carkner, Herbert Gruning, J. Richard Middleton, and Bruce Toombs

Many people think that Christians are too other-worldly and irrelevant to life in modern times. But those who make that claim fail to realize that the Bible emphasizes the value of this world in several ways: (1) in creation, (2) in the incarnation of Jesus, and (3) through salvation. While Christians must be other-worldly because "they envision a world free of evil," they also must have an eye on this world as they oppose evil and work toward healing, love, and justice.

Christians are other-worldly and irrelevant to life in the 20th century.

This accusation often rings true. Many Christians certainly seem other-worldly and even irrelevant. But they do not reflect the main emphasis of the Bible, upon which Christian teaching is founded. Far from being other-worldly, *biblical* Christianity emphasizes the importance of this world in three main ways.

First of all, the Bible claims that the entire universe is created by God and is therefore good and important. Far from negating or devaluing the world, the Bible teaches that God loves his creation and sustains its continued structure and existence. The world exists to manifest God's glory, and he rejoices in what he has made.

But the importance of the world is supported also by the doctrine of the incarnation, the Christian teaching that God became man in Jesus Christ. The authentic humanity of Jesus is constantly affirmed by the Bible. He was not some spiritual manifestation or temporary avatar, but a real life, flesh and blood person.

But why the incarnation? Because creation went wrong. Humanity has chosen evil in rebellion against its Creator, and the world is no longer totally good. Yet God has not given up on us. This is the tremendous message of Christianity. God loves us to the point of becoming a human being to free us from evil, to bring salvation.

The salvation God offers constitutes the third way in which biblical Christianity affirms the importance of this world. Though Christianity is often characterized as a pie-in-the-sky religion, concerned with a hereafter of disembodied existence in an ethereal heaven, this is a gross distortion of its message. There is certainly a future hope of the "kingdom of God." But the Bible describes this kingdom in the most concrete terms. It promises the resurrection of the body and the renewal of the entire creation. Salvation is holistic. Christianity's final vision is of the eradication of evil from the universe. Christ came to restore the creation to what it was meant to be, and that includes every aspect of human (and non-human) life.

This means that there is an important sense in which Christians *must* be other-worldly. Precisely because they envision a world free of evil, both at the beginning and at the end of history, they cannot accept *this* world at face value. They are other-worldly in that they look beyond the distortions and pretensions of this world to the one which is to come. They know there is something better.

But that means that they are fundamentally *this*-worldly. Christians are called upon to oppose evil in all of its individual and socio-cultural manifestations. They work toward healing, love, and justice in this world. In the context of our modern 20th century civilization of violence, oppression, and narcissism, this call is neither other-worldly nor irrelevant.

Questions

1. Why do you think Christians are often accused of being other-worldly and irrelevant? To what degree do you think the description is accurate? Give reasons for your answer.
2. How does the Bible support the view that Christianity is relevant to this world?
3. In what important way must Christians be other-worldly?
4. What are some specific, practical ways that a Christian can "work toward healing, love, and justice in this world"?

Why Should I Believe in a Religion That Causes Oppression?

The Black Past

Tom Skinner

Tom Skinner is a prominent black evangelical who has worked tirelessly to foster racial understanding and coopera-tion between black and white Christians. In this selection from his book How Black Is the Gospel? *Skinner gives a brief overview of the development of the slave system in this country and the role Christianity played in the subjection of blacks. He notes that the exploitation of people cannot be blamed on God, that Jesus would have nothing to do with racism, and that the Bible as the Word of God holds the key to a spiritual revolution.*

Any understanding of the black revolution, any understand-ing of the black man's rage, must come from a knowledge of his violent past. To understand the gospel of Jesus Christ and its implications for the black revolution, we must examine the black man's history. We must go back over the years to 1619, when a ship with no name, with a captain by the name of Jope and an English pilot by the name of Marmaduke, landed in Jamestown, Virginia. That ship began the history of the black man in America—one year before the *Mayflower*. There were approximately twenty black people aboard, and notable among them was a couple known as Isabella and Antony.

These early black settlers were not slaves. In fact, between 1619 and 1660 there was no slave system in the colonies, nor was there any racial inferiority. Our country had what were known as "indentured servants." This system enabled poor white immigrants to sell their services in America for a stipulated number of years. Under this system religious dissenters, ex-convicts, and prostitutes, among others, were brought to the colonies and sold to the highest bidder. These people then worked off the amount paid for them and finally were set free. There were black indentured servants and white indentured servants. Black people held such servants, as well as white people.

During this time, blacks owned land, voted, and testified in court; they held positions of authority; they lived side by side with whites in social and economic equality; they made love to each other and bore children by each other. Kenneth M. Stampp puts it this way: "Negro and white servants of the seventeenth century seemed to be remarkably unconcerned about their visible physical differences. They toiled together in the fields, fraternized during leisure hours, and, in and out of wedlock, collaborated in siring a numerous progeny."

By 1660, with the growth of cotton and tobacco plantations, a larger labor force was needed. The system of indentured servitude could have been continued, but it was expensive. There was the possibility of enslaving the Indians and keeping a free labor system for both blacks and whites. But Indians made poor slaves: they were weak and often sickly and, knowing the countryside so well, found it easy to run away.

All indentured servants might have been enslaved, but this posed problems too. When a white escaped, it was very difficult to recapture him because he could easily blend with the rest of society. Also, white servants tended to be "Christianized." It was very difficult for one Christian to justify enslaving another. Most important, white men were usually the subjects of strong European governments, to which they could appeal for protection.

Black people did not have any of these "disadvantages." They were strong, healthy, visible, cheap, numerous—and unprotected. Thus in Virginia and Maryland in the 1660's, laws were passed making Negroes servants for life. Intermarriage was prohibited, and children of Negro women became bond or free, depending on their mother's condition.

At first, religion was used as an excuse: it was thought to be all right to enslave a non-Christian. Soon even Christianized blacks were made available; in 1667, a Virginia law stated that "the conferring of baptisme does not alter the condition of the person as to his bondage or freedom." Color became the mark of bondage. It was simple from that point on to develop the slave system and to maintain it.

This is one reason that the black community today considers Christianity the white man's religion, given to the black man only in order to keep him in his place. Christianity was used in the Western Hemisphere for many hundreds of years to maintain the white man's economic, political and social control over the black man.

Sixty years after Isabella and Antony landed on American soil, sixty years after black people helped found this country, the European slave trade had reached its height. It is said that Africa lost more than forty million people, half of whom reached the New World. Lerone Bennett, Jr., in his book *Before the Mayflower*, puts it this way:

These figures, though instructive, do not say anything meaningful about the people involved. The slave trade was not a statistic, however astronomical. The slave trade was people living, lying, stealing, murdering and dying. The slave trade was a black man who stepped out of his hut for a breath of fresh air and ended up, ten months later, in Georgia with bruises on his back and a brand on his chest.

The slave trade was a black mother suffocating her new-born baby because she didn't want him to grow up a slave.

The slave trade was a kind captain forcing his suicide-minded passengers to eat by breaking their teeth, though, as he said, he was "naturally compassionate."

The slave trade was a bishop sitting on an ivory chair on a wharf in the Congo and extending his fat hand in wholesale baptism of slaves who were rowed beneath him, going in chains to the slave ships.

The slave trade was a greedy king raiding his own villages to get slaves to buy brandy.

The slave trade was a pious captain holding prayer services twice a day on his slave ship and writing later the famous hymn, "How Sweet the Name of Jesus Sounds."

The slave trade was deserted villages, bleached bones on slave trails and people with no last names.

The slave trade was so prosperous that, by 1710, the number of blacks in the colonies had increased to fifty thousand. By 1776, there were five hundred thousand. By 1860, there were four million black people in America. . . .

Slavery was upheld by three sectors of society: religious, economic, and political. First was the church. Slavery was seen as a divine institution, ordained by God. White pastors throughout the country preached that God had ordained the black man to his condition of servitude. The most quoted story was the incident in the book of Genesis where Noah goes to bed drunk one night. His drunkenness and nakedness is mocked by his son, Canaan. The following morning when Noah discovers what Canaan has done, he curses Canaan. It was argued that Canaan, being a descendant of Ham (Ham meaning Black) was black, and therefore God had cursed all black people and relegated them to a condition of servitude.

Slaves were allowed to have "praying parties," held on Sundays. But what the master allowed to be taught was the virtue of dutiful obedience. One overseer was told that there would be no objection to the slaves hearing the Gospel "in its original purity and simplicity," which meant Ephesians, chapter 6, verse 5: "Servants, be obedient to them that are your masters" (King James Version).

Fortunately, though, not many slaves were deceived by these readings. The God who delivered the Israelites was more meaningful to them. You could hear this coming out of the slave quarters in such songs as "Didn't my Lord deliver Daniel? Then why not every man?" Slaves would slip away into the fields to pour out their troubles to God. There are indications that fantastic spiritual awakenings and revivals took place. "I went down in the valley to pray; my soul got happy and I stayed all day."

Most songs rose from the sorrow and pain of slavery.

I know moon-rise, I know star-rise,
  Lay dis body down.
I walk in de moonlight, I walk in de starlight
  To lay dis body down.
I'll walk in de graveyard, I'll walk through de graveyard
  To lay dis body down.
I'll lie in de grave and stretch out my arms;
  Lay dis body down.
I go to de judgement in de evenin' of de day,
  When I lay dis body down;
And my soul and your soul will meet in de day
  When I lay dis body down.

Hearing this song during the Civil War, Thomas Wentworth Higginson wrote, "Never, it seems to me, since man first lived and suffered, was his infinite longing for peace uttered more plaintively than in that line [the refrain]." . . .

The greatest tragedy in all of the black man's history in this country has been the strange silence of the white church in America. This is not to say that there have been no voices raised in protest. But they have been few and feeble. For the most part, the white church in America has maintained the status quo and upheld the social system. How different from the radical, revolutionary gospel of Bible times, when believers addressed themselves to the roots of injustice and sinful egotism!

The issue that is now before us is: How can an institution which itself has been infested with racism, which has denied black people equality, which has preached a message of separation and segregation, which has sought to use itself to prove that black people were socially, economically and spiritually inferior—how can that church now take a message which it was supposed to have been preaching for all these years and make it relevant to the black community?

Our argument . . . is true that Christianity has never really been applied to the sphere of black-white relations in this country. We therefore set ourselves the task of showing how true Christianity—the real message of Christ—can speak with decisiveness and truth to today's black revolution. . . .

Let's keep in mind that while the white man has used his Christianity to exploit people, you can't blame God for that. And while it is true that there were large segments of the white community which twisted the Bible in order to maintain the slave system, and while it is true that slavery was upheld by the church as a divine institution ordained by God, Jesus Christ never identified Himself with those actions. He was never a part of that. Those were pharisaical, religious hypocrites, who themselves were not really committed to the truth of God's Word, who had never allowed Jesus Christ to be Lord of their lives, but who simply took the religious subculture and used it to maintain and perpetuate their own particular economic and social ends.

You must also admit that it was the penetration of the truth about Scripture that not only sparked within the black man his desire for freedom but motivated him to fight for it. One of the greatest "mistakes" the white man made during the years of slavery was to teach certain slaves to read, and the one book that was read most often was the Bible. There is no other book in all the world that rings with more pride for liberty and justice and freedom and equality. That is what the folksinger meant when be said, "There is a book, and every page rings liberty." Harriet Tubman led more than three hundred black men to freedom through the underground railroad. When she was asked by what means she did it, by what authority she got the right to become involved in leading so many people out of slavery, she stood up and quoted the very Scripture that Jesus Christ quoted in the temple: "The Spirit of the Lord is upon me, because he hath anointed me to preach the gospel to the poor; . . . to preach deliverance to the captives, . . . to set at liberty them that are bruised."

All those people who argue that the message of Jesus Christ has been used to hold black people down are not right. It is true that there were those who twisted the message of the Bible to hold black people in subjugation, but the real message of Jesus Christ—that which speaks of Christ Himself—and people who stood firm in preaching about Him as Lord, kindled fires of freedom and helped bring about the end of slavery. Many of the abolitionists of those early days spoke out as a result of a spiritual revival that came about through the preaching of the Word of God, from the New Testament. The Word of God spoke out against slavery and struck the conscience of a freedom-loving people, the Word of God restored sanity to our people through those dark days of exploitation, the Word of God was the symbol of freedom and justice and equality.

If black people throw out the one weapon that has sustained them for all these years, if we throw away, in this hour of revolution, the one book that has been our guiding light, we are throwing away truth—and there can be no real revolution without truth. Jesus Christ Himself said, "I am the way, and the truth, and the life; no one comes to the Father, but by me." If we do not then deal squarely with the truth, personified in Jesus Christ, if we do not follow His way for living, for true revolution, for real radical change, His way to be real men and real women, His way to the true leadership that our country is in dire need of—if we throw away His truth, which is the person Jesus Christ, our revolution goes the way all other revolutions have gone. If we throw away the Word of God, and the testimony of God through his Son, Jesus Christ, we throw away the life; and we fall into the same trap as our oppressor.

While religion has been part of the institutional establishment, it has been a religion without life. True life comes through Jesus Christ; no man is really alive without Him.

This could be the black man's finest hour, if he could bring to the social, economic and political revolution, a spiritual revolution. For the spiritual revolution precedes all other revolutions; it cannot come later. As the Bible says, "Righteousness exalts a nation, but sin is a reproach to any people."

I have not always been involved with Jesus Christ like that. I have not always been committed to Jesus Christ like that. There was a time when I thought Jesus Christ was a nothing. When I heard about Jesus, I discovered that He was just a carpenter, a man who had banged nails into wooden planks. I checked out His education and I was sure He was nothing. He'd never been to any institution of learning, He had no degrees behind His name, He had never studied at the feet of any of the great philosophers. I did not commit myself to Him because academically He didn't have what it took. He was a nothing. I looked at his dress, and I found out He went around in the dress of common people. He didn't dress in fine linen. He was a nothing.

I pictured Him as a schizophrenic religious leader, so obsessed with Himself that He wanted everybody else to be obsessed with Him. They tried to tell me He was the Son of God, and I decided he was a religious nut. They tried to tell me that He was born of a virgin, and I figured that at best He was an illegitimate child.

And then one day I met Him. I encountered that Christ, and I was overwhelmed by Him! I saw Him as the God of heaven and earth, and I committed my life to him. I now know Him and I count Him to be superior to anything that men can offer. Because of my commitment to Him, I count my family name as garbage, my economic status as garbage, my social position as the dung hill of Jerusalem, that I might know Him and be found in Him. Not having my own righteousness, that I might be discovered in Christ with the righteousness of God. My commitment to Him, my ambition, is to please Him, and to allow Him to flesh Himself out in my black body.

I submit to you that if we can get a glimpse of that kind of commitment in the twentieth century, we can shake our world. May I ask you a personal question? To whom are you committed? Is Jesus Christ more important to you than name? Is Jesus Christ more important to you than family status? Is Jesus Christ more important to you than economic security? Is Jesus Christ more important to you than social status? I will challenge you that there are many of you who are very much dismayed with evangelical Christianity—to the extent that some have copped out on it. And I can't blame you. But what is your alternative? What are you going to replace it with?

I'm simply suggesting that if the evangelical church is irrelevant today, and I believe it is, and if the evangelical church is stale and archaic and impractical, and I believe it is, then the only way we're going to correct it is to return to the Christ of the New Testament. We need to return to that masculine, contemporary, revolutionary Christ who leaps out of the pages of the Bible to call men to Himself. It is only by virtue of our relationship to Him that we're going to change the church structure and make it relevant to the twentieth century.

You will not solve the problem by turning your back on it. You will solve it by returning to the Christ upon whom the church was supposed to have been built in the first place, and allowing Him to be Himself in you, so that you can go out and shake your world.

I wonder if God has spoken to you about being totally committed to Him with no strings attached. Are you prepared to make that commitment to become Christ's revolutionary in the twentieth century? Just say to Jesus Christ, "Lord, here is my life. I give You the right to do with me whatever You please; I give You the right to run my life, and I'm prepared to cut the umbilical cord to anything in order to be totally attached to You, to take my orders directly from You, so that people might in me see You. I'm prepared to be available. I'm prepared to make the sacrifice. I'm prepared to be as radical as You are prepared to be in me. But I'm prepared to let You also be Lord and Master. I'm prepared to take my hands off my life and to stop trying to be what You want and to let You be it for me. I'm tired of trying to be a Christian and getting frustrated with other Christians who are in the same bag. I'm prepared now to be delivered from that bag, to let You be Yourself in me."

All you have to say is, "Lord, I believe that."

Questions

1. What is an indentured servant? How did the indentured servant system work in the early colonial period?
2. What role did the Bible play in the blacks' struggle for freedom from slavery? How and why did it become so influential?
3. Why do you think the Church did not speak out against slavery in the late eighteenth century and early nineteenth century?
4. Why do you think people claim that Christianity causes oppression? How would you counter that claim?

Why Should I Believe in a Religion Invented for Weak People?

"Christianity Is a Crutch for Weak People"

R.C. Sproul

R.C. Sproul is a popular theologian, seminary professor, and author. In this selection he notes that many people feel religion is a psychological crutch. Freud, Marx, and other philosophers believed it, too. Sproul shows that the fundamental questions of Christianity are not psychological, but historical. God has revealed himself to all people through general revelation; however, people by nature are threatened by God.

"Religion is the opiate of the masses." This oft repeated quote from Karl Marx captures a common view of religion. Religion is seen as an attractive intoxicant for the depressed, the downhearted, and the weak. Overpowered by the harsh realities of life, people turn for comfort and emotional support to religion. Religion offers "balm in Gilead" for those who have been brutalized by life. A parallel expression we hear is,

"I don't feel the *need* of religion," as if the truth or falsehood of Christianity depended upon one's feeling of need. At the root of this criticism is the assumption that religion is purely a subjective or emotional matter that involves personal preferences stemming from needs and weaknesses.

In the world of secular philosophy, committed atheists have asked the question, "If there is no God, why are so many people involved in religion?" The atheist seeks to understand where religion came from and why it continues to persist in an enlightened age if there is no objective and real foundation for its existence. The most common answer is that man invents God out of the pressures of human fears and weaknesses.

Was Religion Invented to Tame Natural Forces?

The father of modern psychoanalysis, Sigmund Freud, was very much interested in discovering the answer to the question of the origin of religion. He proposed a very interesting and credible theory on the motives behind the human invention of religion.

The threat of nature which holds many mysteries and displays awesome powers of destructive force is "tamed" by postulating a God who can help men in the struggles of life. Freud says:

> There are the elements, which seem to mock at all human control: the earth, which quakes and is torn apart and buries all human life and its works; water, which deluges and drowns everything in a turmoil; storms, which blow everything before them; there are diseases, which we have only recently recognized as attacks by other organisms; and finally there is the painful riddle of death, against which no medicine has yet been found, nor probably will be. With these forces nature rises up against us, majestic, cruel and inexorable; she brings to our mind once more our weakness and helplessness, which we thought to escape through the work of civilization.

Given the threat of nature, Freud sees man going through a process of humanizing and personalizing nature. Religion begins by attributing human characteristics and personality to impersonal forces such as earthquakes and storms. If a human being is angry with me and threatens to harm me, I can do several things to dissuade him. I can plead for mercy; I can flatter and praise him to try to get him to like me; I can offer to provide services for him if he treats me kindly; I can try to bribe him. There are a host of ways to deal with human anger. We understand personal anger because we deal with it every day. But how do you negotiate with a hurricane? You can't bribe it or plead with it to go away. It has no checking account and no ears to hear your pleas for mercy. Freud answers that man deals with the impersonal forces of nature by personalizing them via religion. You invent a spirit that lives in the storm or the flood. If the spirits are personal then all the forces of personal persuasion can be brought to bear on them. From a simple form of animistic spirit-powers inhabiting nature, man develops a more sophisticated religion of monotheism. In the monotheism all the pleading, bargaining, praise, and service can be focused on one personal deity who has control of all nature. The ultimate crutch then becomes a personal God, a combination of kindly grandfather, cosmic bellhop, and celestial bodyguard. By religion, nature is made sacred and personal so that its threatening power is brought under control.

Is Religion an Invention of the Rich?

Karl Marx explains the origin and function of religion in economic terms. It is not so much the hurricane that provokes religious interest as it is the cruel forces of economic conflict. Marx sees religion as the invention of the controlling economic classes. The ruling classes are in a minority, and they accumulate an inordinate amount of wealth. With wealth and luxury in the hands of a few, the rich, he says, are always afraid of an uprising by the poor masses. If the masses ever find out how much collective power they have and revolt against the rich, the rich are in trouble. So how does the minority control the majority? They invent a religion that does several things to protect their vested interests. The religion emphasizes such virtues as industry, service, humility, and obedience. This religious "ethic" helps keep the masses in line.

The religion also provides comfort and consolation to the weak and needy and gives a kind of "spiritual" dignity to the oppressed. The big prize that religion offers the workers is the promise of pie-in-the-sky in the next life. If the worker refrains from violent revolution and the love of money in this life, God will reward him with milk and honey and streets of gold in heaven. In the meantime, the rich enjoy their milk, honey, and gold right now. The ethic and the promise keep the masses intoxicated with a kind of opium. They are drugged by religion and kept in a kind of euphoric stupor while the rich continue to exploit them.

Other similar theories of the origin of religion have been set forth by Nietzsche, Feuerbach, Russell, Sartre, and others. Though the theories differ in points of detail, they contain a common element of argumentation. The idea that religion owes its origin and its sustaining power to psychological needs runs as a common thread through all of them.

A few important things must be said at the outset of any serious response to these theories and objections. There is no dispute that man has the power of creative imagination and the capacity to turn his fantasies into theories or full-blown religious systems. It must also be admitted that man does find in religion an important resource for comfort and consolation. That people are often attracted to religion by emotional needs is not in dispute. That religion has been used countless times in history as a tool of exploitation is not in dispute. But the same thing can be said for atheism.

There are profound psychological reasons that motivate people toward the rejection of religion. Being mistreated by a priest, disillusioned by a "religious" parent (as Marx was), being exploited by a religious charlatan, can all be subjective motives for the rejection of faith. The atheist has his vested interests too. A man burdened by serious guilt may want very much for there to be no God. A man wanting to indulge his own desires at the expense of others may like the idea that he is not ultimately accountable to a just and holy God.

If There Is No God Why Is There Religion?

The theories of the origin of religion set forth by Freud and the others offer no proof or falsification of the case of theism. The nonexistence of God is assumed. Their question is, "If there is no God why is there religion?" If indeed there is no God then their theories of the origin of religion are plausible. But first it must be established that in fact there is no God. That man has the ability to invent religion is obvious. That he in fact did invent religion is not so obvious.

In a courtroom in criminal trial the question of means and motive are relevant. If the prosecutor can prove that the accused had the means to commit the crime and a strong motive for doing it, this helps his case. If the defense can prove that his client had neither means nor motive, it goes a long way to establish his innocence. But the prosecutor must prove more than the means and the motive of the defendant. He must show evidence that the accused actually did commit the crime. If a person is murdered, a large number of people could be found who had the means and motive to commit murder.

The question of the origin of religion (or the origin of anything) is not fundamentally a psychological question but an historical one. Psychology plays a definite role but cannot be the decisive factor in determining what in fact did happen in the past. If the believer has only one argument for the existence of God—namely, that the existence of religion proves the existence of God—then the Freudian hypothesis would be devastating. Indeed it would be strange if there were a God and no one believed in Him, but the presence of believers or absence of believers could not determine the issue by itself. It is both theoretically possible that there be a God with no one believing in Him and that there is no God while everyone believes He exists. The truth of reality is not determined by counting noses.

Though the atheist offers an interesting study of psychological motives for religious belief, he must also recognize that
the New Testament offers some interesting input about the
psychological motives for atheism.

The apostle Paul offers a counteroffensive to the atheist in
his Epistle to the Romans. He says:

> For the wrath of God is revealed from heaven against all
> ungodliness and wickedness of men who by their wicked-
> ness suppress the truth (Rom. 1:18).

Paul elaborates his theme of general revelation arguing
that God has clearly revealed Himself to all men through the
created order. He maintains that all men "clearly perceive" this
revelation. However man "represses" or "suppresses" this
knowledge. The word he uses is the (Greek term *katakein*. This
word has been translated variously by "stifle," "hold down,"
"suppress," "repress," and "hinder." J.H. Bavinck writes:

> It seems to me that in this case we should translate it by
> "repress." We intentionally choose a word which has a spe-
> cific meaning in psychological literature. *Webster's New
> Collegiate Dictionary* defines "repression" as the "process by
> which unacceptable desires or impulses are excluded from
> consciousness and thus being denied direct satisfaction are
> left to operate in the unconscious." This seems to agree
> with what Paul says here about human life. But we must
> mention that the word repression has received a wider
> meaning in more recent psychology. In Freudian psycholo-
> gy it specifically refers to unconscious desires of a more or
> less sexual nature. In more recent psychology it is also
> applied to desires or impulses of a very different nature.
> The impulses or desires which are repressed may be very
> valuable. Any thing that goes contrary to the accepted pat-
> terns of life or to the predominant popular ideas may be
> repressed. Usually this happens and results can be far-
> reaching. We are reminded of this psychological phe-

nomenon recently discovered by Paul's use of the word. He says that man always naturally represses God's truth because it is contrary to his pattern of life.

Thus Paul says that man receives a clear revelation from God but represses that truth and refuses to acknowledge what he knows to be true. He has a negative psychological reaction to the knowledge of God. There is a sense in which the knowledge of God is traumatic to people. It provokes fear and dread.

Paul goes on to say in the same context that man "exchanges the truth of God for a lie and serves the creature rather than the Creator" (see Rom. 1:23). This exchange or "substitution" of idolatry for authentic religion indicates that the repressed knowledge is not actually destroyed. In traumatic experiences the memory is not obliterated but forced down into the unconscious. The "knowledge" is not destroyed and will work its way back to the surface in veiled or disguised forms. Psychiatrists in treating patients pay close attention not only to the words that are spoken but to the nonverbal actions that accompany the words. When a patient has a noticeable "tic" every time his mother is mentioned, the doctor knows this is significant. Dream interpretation is another means of exploring veiled and disguised memory images.

Translating this to religious terms we see that man has a propensity to soften his understanding of God by creating images of God in religious garb that are nonthreatening. It is common for people to speak of belief in "higher power" or as "something greater than ourselves." These faceless, nameless deities are abstractions which make no personal demands upon us. "Religion" may represent human attempts to tame God or remove the threat of His truth from us. It is one thing to believe in a "higher power"; it is another to believe in a holy personal God who makes ultimate demands upon us and before whom we are ultimately accountable. To postulate the belief in a nebulous "higher power" is to hedge a bit between atheism and a full-bodied Christianity with its personal demands.

Why Are We Afraid of God?

If Paul is correct and it is true that God has revealed Himself to all men, what is it about Him that would terrify us so much and lead us into this exchange-substitution process? There is much about God that can evoke negative feelings of terror. Perhaps the five most significant aspects of His being that make us uncomfortable are: 1) His holiness, 2) His omniscience, 3) His sovereignty, 4) His omnipotence, and 5) His immutability.

The threat of holiness. Rudolf Otto did a massive study of the effect on people of various cultures of the experience of the holy. He discovered that mankind from the Fiji Islands to Washington, D.C. have a strong sense of ambivalence to the holy. Mixed feelings of dread and fascination seem to accompany such experiences. The biblical record uniformly relates that when men confront the holy they are reduced to a state of terror.

The prophet Isaiah recorded his experience in the Temple of encountering a vision of the Holy God of Israel. The effect of the experience was a threat of disintegration.

> In the year that King Uzziah died I saw the Lord sitting upon a throne, high and lifted up; and his train filled the temple. Above him stood the seraphim; each had six wings: with two he covered his face, and with two he covered his feet, and with two he flew. And one called to another and said: "Holy, holy, holy is the LORD of hosts; the whole earth is full of his glory." And the foundations of the thresholds shook at the voice of him who called, and the house was filled with smoke. And I said: "Woe is me! For I am lost; for I am a man of unclean lips, and I dwell in the midst of a people of unclean lips; for my eyes have seen the King, the LORD of hosts!" (Isa. 6:1-5).

What does Isaiah mean when he says that he is "undone" (KJV) after beholding the vision of the holiness of God? If we translate this word into contemporary categories of speech we could describe it in terms of the psychological process of disintegration. Isaiah is "coming apart" or "breaking down." His self-image is shattered and his sense of wholeness or integration is annihilated. Why? Where formerly he judged himself by comparing himself to other fallen human beings and thus came to a high opinion of himself, he now measures himself against the ultimate standard of holiness. In the vision experience Isaiah not only finds out who God is, but he also finds out who Isaiah is. His self-image is shattered as he sees himself as a man of unclean lips. The same experience of personal disintegration is recorded by Job and by the prophet Habakkuk.

Another strange example of men's reaction to the holy may be seen in the biblical incident of Jesus' stilling the tempest:

> And leaving the crowd, they took him with them, just as he was, in the boat. And other boats were with him. And a great storm of wind arose, and the waves beat into the boat, so that the boat was already filling. But he was in the stern, asleep on the cushion; and they woke him and said to him, "Teacher, do you not care if we perish?" And he awoke and rebuked the wind, and said to the sea, "Peace! Be still!" And the wind ceased, and there was a great calm. He said to them, "Why are you afraid? Have you no faith?" And they were filled with awe, and said to one another, "Who then is this, that even the wind and the sea obey him?" (Mark 4:36-41).

Here we have a unique combination of a description of men's fear of the power of nature coupled with the human fear of the holy. Note that the narrative speaks of the fishermen's fear of the sudden tempest. Yet, after the tempest has ceased and the sea is calmed they become "very much afraid." When the threat of nature is removed their fear is not eliminated but increased. Now they are more afraid of Jesus than they were of the storm. They say, "Who then is this?" Other translations read, "What manner of man is this?" There was no safe category in which they could put Jesus and disarm Him. He was in a class by Himself, a class that was utterly alien—the class of the Holy.

The same response is expressed by Peter after Jesus has his nets filled to the breaking point following a frustrating night of fishing without success. Instead of asking Jesus to go into the fishing business with him, Peter exclaims, "Depart from me, for I am a sinful man, O Lord" (Luke 5:8). Peter articulates a common human desire, that we be removed to a safe distance from the Holy.

At this point I must challenge Freud's thesis that the fear of nature is the chief factor in the origin of Christianity. To be sure the personal non-holy is less threatening than the impersonal non-holy. But what about the personal Holy? Man may indeed invent a personal deity to protect him from nature. But would he invent a personal Holy deity whose holiness is even more dreadful than the forces of nature?

The threat of omniscience. One of our greatest fears in this life is that our most closely-guarded secrets might be exposed. We like privacy and choose our intimate confidants very carefully. There are closely guarded skeletons in everybody's closet. The specter of an Orwellian "big brother" who observes our every move is most unpopular. Jean Paul Sartre has written extensively of the feeling of "shame-consciousness" that goes with the experience of being watched through a keyhole. The biblical imagery of "nakedness" calls attention to the same discomfort of shame. The first awareness of man after the Fall was expressed not in overt terms of guilt but in an awareness of nakedness. The first action of man after the Fall was to hide himself from the gaze of God.

If God is omniscient then every closet is transparent. There is nowhere to hide. He cannot be deceived or avoided; there can be no cover-up. Again and again the cry of the biblical character caught in the grips of personal guilt is that God should not look at him. When we commit acts of evil we do not want God to look at us but to overlook us. Kierkegaard said, "Man lives incognito throughout his life."

That man fears the gaze of an omniscient God is an important part of the background for the biblical notion of the cross.

The New Testament frequently speaks of the righteousness of Christ serving as a "covering" for man. If we are uncomfortable in our moral nakedness, we can go to Christ for a cover or we can seek to deny that anybody is at the keyhole.

The threat of sovereignty. If anything about God provokes negative psychological reactions, it is His law. Over against all of our self-interests stands the absolute law of God. If there is a God, then I am not free to do as I please. I may have a measure of freedom, but I can never be autonomous. I can never have an absolute license to "do my own thing." But if there is no God then, as Dostoyevsky said, "All things are permissible." Thus God's sovereignty is on a collision course with my own evil desires. The primordial temptation offered by the serpent was, "You will not die, but you shall be as gods" (see Gen. 3:5). But if God is, I cannot ever be a god. The desire for absolute freedom is strong in the corrupt heart of man. To achieve such freedom God must be destroyed or denied. The nebulous "higher power" is a God without sovereignty, a God without a law.

The problem of guilt is one of the most paralyzing factors in human life. Any psychiatrist knows how devastating guilt can be to the human personality. But when real guilt is acquired there are basically two things we can do about it. We can deny it, or we can seek to have it forgiven. The first alternative seems to be the least painful, but it doesn't work. The guilt is real and requires real forgiveness. At the heart of the attempt of man to deny the existence of guilt is the urgent need of man to be free of his guilt. If we get rid of God, we get rid of guilt.

The attempt to circumvent the sovereignty of God and be free of guilt takes subtle forms. Not everyone forcefully denies the existence of God. Rather God's nature is reshaped into a deity whose only attribute is love. God is stripped of His wrath, justice, and sovereignty; He is left clad only with a maudlin kind of love that makes no demands. This kind of God requires no repentance but exhibits a kind of love that means "never having to say that you are sorry." This stripped, weak, helpless God is the God of a very popular American religion. But it is not Christianity.

The threat of omnipotence. Power is one of the most intimidating devices that men exploit to gain their goals. The carrying of a "big stick" can provoke great fear. Policemen have nicknamed their nightsticks "persuaders." They know that instruments of force produce a certain psychological response. If we tremble at a nightstick which represents limited, finite power how much more intimidated are we by one who rules with absolute power. He is sometimes called a "higher" power, but why isn't He referred to as an "absolute power"? Even the term "higher power" represents an attempt to escape the absolute character of God's power.

This attribute of God is enough in itself to provoke a prejudicial vote for atheism. Perhaps we fear that God's absolute power will be wielded against us in a tyrannical way. We hear that power corrupts and that absolute power corrupts absolutely. In saying that we forget that with God absolute power is coupled with absolute holiness. (Maybe that is why we fear it so much.) When we add to that absolute power, absolute holiness, absolute omniscience, and absolute sovereignty, we are overwhelmed. In contrast to God I am impotent. Atheism, however, gives me the opportunity "kick sand in the face of God."

The threat of immutability. Why would the unchanging character of God be an attribute that threatens us? This attribute cannot be viewed in isolation from the rest. In relationship to God's other attributes this one is the clincher. For with God's immutability all hope that God will ever change vanishes. There is no hope that tomorrow God will compromise His holiness. There is no chance that God will ever fall and become tainted with sin as we are. There is not the remotest possibility that God will be afflicted with a hardening of the arteries and begin to have lapses of memory. His eyesight will never become dim so we can escape His gaze. His omnipotence will never be diminished by muscle atrophy and feebleness. His sovereignty will never be overthrown by a coup d'etat. Whatever God is now, He will be forever. Thus, if I am going to get along with God, it is I who must change, not He.

God reveals Himself to us as a formidable opponent. He

evokes such feelings of dread within us that our reasoning about Him might easily be clouded. Religion, indeed, might be used as a crutch; but the atheist must also acknowledge that the crutch might be needed for the other foot.

It must be said that pointing out the possible reasons why prejudice can be a factor in religious conclusions is not enough to demonstrate the existence of God. Being aware of these potential and actual points of prejudice is important to the discussion on both sides. When we are dealing with the question of the existence of God, we are dealing with an issue in which we all have an ultimate vested interest. No one can deal with the question with a totally dispassionate attitude; there is too much as stake. There are times when we need to "train the guns" on ourselves to check our own vested interests. The most devout Christian may have already allowed his own prejudices to soften his view of God. Let us deal with the biblical God on the terms in which He is presented in the Bible. If we reshape Him and "create Him in our own image" then we will have obscured His real identity. The truth can never be determined by what we want it to be. God may, in fact, be everything we want Him to be, but if that is so, it is not because He shapes Himself according to our desires. If He is, He is what He is in and by Himself. If He is not, all my desires about Him are impotent ant futile.

The question of Christianity and truth cannot be affirmed or denied simply by examining human need and prejudice. Prejudice works on both sides of the issue. If I feel the need of religion, that cannot validate its claims. If I do not feel the need of religion, that does not negate or falsify its claims.

Key Points to Remember

Is Christianity a crutch for weak people?

1. *We all need a crutch.* In a sense we must agree that Christianity is a crutch for weak people. But because we are all crippled, it is a crutch we all need. The question is, does the crutch have any basis in reality or is it an artificially devised aid? Do we "invent" God because we need Him?

2. *Psychological needs may prompt us to invent God.* We must admit to the Freuds and Sartres of this world that we do want there to be a God and that we would be capable of inventing "God" even if there was none. We must acknowledge that there are many things about life that threaten us, such as the force of nature, the danger of disease, and the inevitable threat of death.

3. *Psychological needs may also prompt us to deny God.* God is a threat to us too. Atheism may also be positioned as a crutch motivated by a desire to escape the judgment of God. The atheist must acknowledge that the crutch may be for the "other foot."

4. *The biblical God is more threatening than nature itself.*

5. *God's holiness, omniscience, sovereignty, omnipotence, and immutability make Him an awesome threat to us* (see Ps. 38:1-4).

6. *Even Christians "water-down" the character of the biblical God.* The Christian God is "awesome" and we frequently water-down His character within the Christian church.

7. *The truth of Christianity cannot be determined by psychology.* A study of human needs and prejudices teach us a lot about ourselves but nothing about whether or not God really exists. We must note the crucial difference between the question of how religion *could have* started and how it, in fact, *did* start.

Questions

1. Describe Freud's view concerning the origin of religion. Describe the Marxist view of religion.
2. Why do people use terms like "higher power" or "something greater than ourselves"? How do these terms "tame" God?
3. What attributes of God evoke feelings of terror in people? What do these attributes tell you about God? Why do they evoke feelings of terror in people?

Is Christianity a Crutch?

Michael Green

Michael Green admits that Christianity is a "repair religion" for imperfect people living in an imperfect world. In that sense, it is a crutch. But most people making this accusation, including Sigmund Freud, mean that it's nothing more than a psychological illusion. Green counters by claiming that Christianity is authenticated by the tests of history, character, and power.

"I don't need Christianity. It's just a crutch for weaklings."

I have often heard a sneer like that. I sometimes wonder how the young person, full of health and scorn, who utters those words, would feel if he went skiing in the Alps and broke his leg. I wonder if his attitude towards crutches might change?

A rescue religion

In one sense, Christianity *is* a crutch. It is for people who are fractured. If ours were a perfect world and if we were perfect people there would be no need for Christianity. But such is not the case. Our world, our lives are fractured by greed and selfishness, lust and cruelty. Don't believe me. Just watch the news or read a newspaper. Christianity is unashamedly a repair religion. It is not for the healthy but for the sick: that's what Jesus said. He knew that there are no healthy. "There is none righteous, no, not one." Not even you.

So in this sense Christianity is a crutch. It is designed to enable the incapacitated to walk, the greedy to become generous, the lonely integrated, the miserable happy. And Christians maintain that the wood of which that crutch is fashioned will bear anyone's weight. It is well seasoned. It has been maturing for two thousand years. We shall examine the evidence for that claim later on.

An illusion?

But this crutch argument can have a very different twist to it. The claim is not that Christianity is a crutch in the sense of a support: there is none of us so healthy that we do not need that support, and one of the glories of the Christian church is that it is both a hospital and an army. No, when they say that Christianity is just a crutch they mean that it is puerile, illusory, an imaginary solace for the neurotic, an opiate which is designed to discourage social action.

That is the claim, and it has never been put more forcefully and influentially than by Freud. He wrote several books about it, the most trenchant being *The Future of an Illusion*. Freud regarded the Christian religion as a crutch in the sense of something illusory. It did not correspond to anything in the real world. Christianity had the status of an obsessional neurosis. Christians show the classic neurotic tendency to find comfort in religion, and to seek an authority figure. They project into the empty heavens a Father-figure derived from their own youth. Such belief is the crutch for weaklings and neurotics. It is an illusion, and it arises from subconscious need for comfort and protection.

Freud's position is exposed to a number of criticisms and has been rejected in general by experts in the field of psychology and the behavioural sciences. But it has been readily accepted by the man in the street and by intelligent people in the arts.

Yes, the man in the street has the impression that Freud has explained Christianity away. But has he? There are certainly neurotic Christians, just as there are neurotic psychiatrists. Some Christians are as obsessive about God as Freud was about sex. However, Freud's assumption that God does not exist, but is the projection of our wishful—or fevered—imagination, needs to be evaluated. His complete neglect of the historical basis of Christianity is most surprising. His generalizations, based on a sample which consisted entirely of the mentally ill, are neither scientific nor convincing. Moreover he isolates those elements in Christianity which fit his theory and neglects others, like love of neighbour, which do not. That makes me uneasy. How about you?

Freud has nevertheless put his finger on a most important issue. Is God an illusion? Is the whole of the Christian story pious make believe? How are we to tell?

. . . Now it may be that Freud and those who follow him are right in supposing that the Christian belief in the fatherly love of God is a reversion to our childhood father-image which we project into the empty heavens. On the other hand it may be the case that there is a God and that he is best described as Father. Let us try to assess these two answers by applying certain tests. Here are three which seem appropriate.

The test of history

Christianity is a historical religion. To dispose of it, you must first get rid of or explain away its founder. And that is a very difficult thing to do. Various theories have been propounded which attempt to explain Jesus as a myth, but they will not stand up to sharp historical investigation. The folly of all such attempts to sidestep the historical Jesus was exposed long ago by Sir James Frazer, author of *The Golden Bough*. He was no friend to Christianity, yet he wrote:

The doubts which have been cast on the historical reality of Jesus are in my judgement unworthy of serious attention. Quite apart from the positive evidence of history, the origin of a great moral and religious reform is incredible without the personal existence of a great reformer. To dissolve the founder of Christianity into a myth is as absurd as to do the same with Mohammed, Luther or Calvin.

But granted the historicity of Jesus, what are we to make of him? His impact on the world was no illusion. We even date our era from his birth. His life of love and integrity, of courage and insight, unparalleled in the annals of mankind, is no illusion. There is nothing illusory about his claims to share God's nature and character: these claims are widely attested in the documents that have come down to us. They are either true or sheer megalomania. His death was real enough, on the rough gibbet of a Roman cross. The resurrection is examined elsewhere in this book, and it is very hard indeed to dub that as illusory. And certainly nobody could deny the reality of the Christian church. That church sprang into being in the thirties of the first century. Its basic message has not changed, and it has gained adherents in increasing millions down the centuries since then, spreading out into every country and tribe in the world—and most strongly in countries like China and Russia where the opposition is most fierce.

In short, there is no lack of evidence about Jesus of Nazareth. His influence and his followers are very much alive all over the world. The Christian religion is based firmly and squarely upon him. The idea that Christianity is wish-fulfillment or self-delusion is shipwrecked on the solid rock of the historical Jesus.

The test of character

The second test of the validity of Christian experience is character. Wherever this faith has appeared across the world and down the ages it has had the most remarkable effects on the character of those who practised it. It has turned rakes into saints, cheats into honest men, enemies into brothers. It would be remarkable if an illusion produced this effect occasionally; but when you find the same results occurring all the time wherever the gospel goes, irrespective of the background, the intelligence and the nationality of the people concerned, then you have every reason to regard what causes the change as real.

An interesting testimony to this transformation of character comes from a surprising source, Charles Darwin. Commending the work of one Mr. Fegan, a preacher in his own village, Darwin said, "Your services have done more for the village in a few months than all our efforts for many years. We have never been able to reclaim a single drunkard, but through your services I do not know that there is a drunkard left in the village!" As a matter of fact he went a good deal further than this. When he first visited Tierra del Fuego he found the savagery and bestiality of the native inhabitants to be beyond belief. When, some years later, he returned, he was amazed at the difference. During his absence a Christian mission had been at work. The people were transformed by the gospel of Jesus Christ and its social and moral implications. And Darwin became a contributor to that missionary society for the rest of his life.

I was recently in America alongside a clergyman who works in the bars and brothels of an inner-city ghetto. We were leading to Christ one of the really tough customers there who had been resisting the gospel for two years. It was a moving experience. But I could not help thinking of the story of the clergyman himself. When I first met him some years ago he was out of work, estranged from his wife, a severe alcoholic, a chain-smoker, sleeping around with prostitutes, and full of bitterness. In the pit of despair this man turned to Jesus Christ. The transformation is plain for all to see. Try persuading him it is illusory!

If you go to the countries of Peru and Colombia, where the Quechua Indians live, you will see a remarkable thing. That large tribe has the reputation for indolence and fecklessness. Until 1956 they were utterly impervious to all attempts to reach them with the gospel of Christ. But since that date many thousands of them have become believers. The results are startling. They begin to take a pride in their families and homes. They begin to work the land and to bring water to their villages. Drunkenness and adultery have almost disappeared. Literacy has grown, and love and laughter have come in. The government officials have noted the difference with profound respect. That is simply one example of the character-change which the gospel of Jesus Christ always produces when he is allowed to control the life. Illusion? A crutch? The idea is laughable.

The test of power

This brings us naturally to the third test of the validity of religious experience, the test of power. All that we know about delusions and obsessional neuroses is that they tend towards the disintegration of character, unbalanced behaviour and either the inability to achieve goals, or else the dissipation of energy in some strange byway of living. But Christianity has precisely the opposite effect. It makes people whole.

I think of a person deep in black magic who is now, through the liberation afforded by Christ, free from all that and has become a very different person. I think of radiant Christian believers in Uganda, freed from the hatred of a terrible dictator like President Amin who murdered so many of their families and friends. One who escaped that holocaust by a hair's breadth, Bishop Festo Kivengere, can write a book entitled *I Love Idi Amin* and return to his country to encourage forgiveness and partnership all round. I think of a Christian who had been unjustly imprisoned on Robin Island in South Africa, yet remained full of goodwill to those who put him there. I think of Maasai and Kikuyu in Northern Kenya, hereditary enemies: but those who have become Christians are treating each other as brothers. I think of a man trained for ordination in a college where I used to work. He was not long out of prison, and had a variety of chips on his shoulder. Now he is a happy, integrated and most effective clergyman on a tough housing estate. I think of President Nixon's famous aide, Chuck Colson, who found Christ shortly before the Watergate scandal broke, then pleaded guilty and served his sentence in prison. Colson is now giving his life to reclaiming prisoners for Christ throughout the United States, taking them away in small groups to Fellowship House in Washington, and helping them to go back into their prisons to start Christian groups there. Christianity like that seems to me to pass the test of power with flying colours. There is no illusion, no crutch about it.

Questions

1. What three tests does Green put forth to support the truth of the Christian religion?
2. Why is a historical test useful? What does it prove?
3. How does Christianity affect personal character? Can you think of someone from your own experience whose character was changed by encountering Christ?
4. Why is the "test of power" a convincing argument?

Finding Wholeness

George Carey

George Carey is the Archbishop of Canterbury, a prominent leader in the Church. In this selection, Carey writes of the need people have for God. That need may be met in various ways—through the intellect, through personal transformation, through the experience of a friend. But he says that we should never consider people who need God to be inadequate. On the contrary, Christianity is that element which brings wholeness and integration to a person's life.

We must say something about "needing God." It is sometimes said that the presence of religion in the world—which even the most jaundiced agnostic will admit to be extremely prevalent in human history and shows no sign of diminishing—is merely a psychological crutch that reassures insecure people that they are not alone. This way of explaining religion, which started with Feuerbach, journeyed into Marxism, was continued by Freud, and has become folklore with some sophisticates, should be dismissed by all thinking people. To be sure, there will always be those who will need crutches, and a faith supplies this for some. But for the vast majority of Christians such a suggestion is an insult and an inadequate explanation for the presence of faith in God.

On the contrary, a number of things can be said about need. We can say with Philip Toynbee, the journalist, for example, that "It is true that the need is no proof that God exists; but it is at least a suggestive and interesting element in many people's composition. Strange creatures, if we felt so strong a need for something which was never there." Of course, we must not push this too far because not everyone feels the urge to worship or that it is necessary to postulate the existence of a

Being beyond them. Nevertheless, the idea expressed so beautifully in Ecclesiastes 3:11 that "Thou hast set eternity in man's heart" captures something of our restless drive for a divinity that eludes us. The presence of religion since the beginning of time—indeed, some would argue that it is the thing that makes humankind distinctively human—is a factor that cannot easily be brushed aside. And that was Toynbee's point, that the universal striving for "something" beyond us cannot simply be explained by appealing to wish fulfillment.

Furthermore, when we use the word "need," we inevitably give it a narrow meaning of "hunger for God." We find it difficult ever to imagine ourselves saying as some Christians do, "I reached rock bottom, my life was falling apart, and Jesus rescued me. I felt suicidal and he was there to help." And, perhaps, we find ourselves thinking, "That's fine for you, but what a neurotic mess you were in the first place! That's not for me!" Men, especially, are prone to despise anything that they think is "weak." Now it is true that God meets that kind of need. Many have found God at points of crises in their lives when God stepped in at the nick of time. But not all Christians find their way to faith through that kind of need. I did not, and I suspect that the majority do not. We need to give breadth to the idea of "needing God." The kind of breadth I have in mind is caught so well in Augustine's famous saying: "Our hearts are restless until they rest in thee." That is to say, that at the heart of every human self some form of encounter with God is required that is akin to "coming home," "finding oneself," to becoming fully what we are. And the ways into this center are so varied and diverse that we can only pick out some of the more popular pathways.

There is the God who makes intellectual sense for us and who becomes the center of our way of looking at life. For many, the Christian way is not the meeting of an emotional need, but a wonderful way of seeing the world through companionship with the Maker. So the poet and writer George MacDonald spoke so revealingly about water: "Is oxygen and hydrogen the divine idea of Water? God put the two together only that man might separate and find them out? He allows his child to pull his toys to pieces; but were they made that he might pull us to pieces? . . . Find for us what is in the constitution of the two gases, makes them fit and capable to be thus honoured in forming the lovely thing, and you will give us a revelation about more than water, namely about the God who makes oxygen and hydrogen. There is no water in oxygen, no water in hydrogen; it comes bubbling fresh from the imagination of the living God, rushing from the great white throne of the glacier . . . Let him who would know the truth of the Maker, become sorely athirst and drink of the brook by the way—then lift up his heart—not at that moment to the Maker of oxygen and hydrogen, but to the Inventor and Mediator of thirst and water, that man might foresee a little his soul might find in God." Such beautiful words express the poetry of science, which is lost once we strip the divine from life.

Then there are those whose need of God has come through the transformation of life. Finding God has led to a total reordering of mind, emotions, and body in which true "wholeness" has come. They felt quite integrated as people before but now, *all* is well. Somehow the missing link has been found, uniting all the diverse parts of their personality and experience. I can think of a senior scientist in one of our leading universities whose discovery of the Christian faith revolutionized his emotional life, thus freeing a rigid and somewhat cold personality, resulting not only in the deepening of his personal relationships but also leading to a love of music and art.

Finally, there are those for whom faith has come through its effect on other people—friends, family, or acquaintances. So impressed have they been that they themselves have traveled towards God. For them, "need" describes what they were missing before. "I had no idea," they might say, "that Christianity could give me such joy or such peace. What I glimpsed through my friend's testimony, I have discovered for myself and what a difference it makes!" What I am saying then is that, in such ways, our need of God comes not simply through psychological need, but through an awareness that without God we have not reached our true stature and destiny. Like most discoveries we only discover what the treasure really is when we find it. That is why those outside the circle always find it so hard to understand what it is that insiders talk about because as yet they cannot share those concerns. Once in, we find the reality that has eluded us—the reality for which we have been searching for years.

[Another] thing that needs to be said about need is that we must refute the idea that those who need God are somehow inadequate people. No doubt some of us are—whether we are Christians or not. None of us can claim to have advanced to full maturity, or complete humanity, and we would no doubt approve of Charles Spurgeon's wry comment about a man in his congregation: "We all thought our brother was perfect until he told us so!" However, there are a surprising number of people who are not only convinced Christians but are also professional people in society, serving as doctors, teachers, solicitors, scientists, lecturers, government leaders, and so on. Not only is this so, but we expect, and often find, that the reality of faith is reflected in changed lives. Any experienced minister will look for signs of God's blessing in a person's life and will find it if faith is genuine. We expect that person to be different. We expect people to grow as persons, to become more mature, more self-reliant and able to cope with life's problems. The tree is undoubtedly known by its fruits, but the tree has to be there to begin with.

And this last point gets to the heart of what Christian faith is all about. It is not a kind of armor that protects inadequate and scared people who have no resources of their own. It is a way of life that is given by God and that makes us the kind of people God wants us to be. An illustration of the illusions some people have about the Christian life is reflected in a letter written by a man to the theologian Dr. J.S. Whale some years ago: "I am 65 years of age, retired after an active life and very happy. My wife is six months younger than me. We have been married forty years very happily. We have never attended church. We have never said a prayer. We neither believe in life after death. We believe in making this world better. Without

being egotistical I believe that we have succeeded. We are highly respected by our neighbours, we are not hampered by any
creeds but stare life squarely in the face. You might in your
talks tell me what religion has to offer us."

I have no idea how Dr. Whale replied, but essentially here
is a self-satisfied man who has already made up his mind that
he does not need God. No one would deny his good life, but
he does not consider it possible that he could be better, that
conceivably he might learn something from a faith tested by
millions down the centuries, that he could be wrong! I would
guess that for such a man the challenge of Christianity will not
come, to begin with, in addition but in subtraction; his pride
and self-sufficiency must yield before the claims of almighty
God. He must see himself not as superior to Christians he
knows, or religious systems he despises, but alongside Jesus
Christ. Once there he will begin to see himself in a different
light and begin to discover that what he lacks is not a collection of moral qualities but a relationship to a person.

I am persuaded that what modern people need above all
else is an holistic approach to life. Have you noticed the tendency for us to add things on? "It'll be nice to have a bit of religion," we think, and so we start going to church occasionally or
we read something uplifting. The mental attitude appears to be
politics plus religion, or music plus religion, or science plus religion, and by adding things we still subconsciously separate
these disciplines into different worlds. But without God there is
no wonder, no science, no music, no beauty, no space, and no
art. It is not a question of adding faith on to what is there but,
rather, allowing faith to transform what is already there, letting
it transfuse and irradiate what are God's gifts to us.

Once we begin to see our "need" in terms of wholeness,
we begin to approach the issue of Christianity in a wholly new
way and see it in terms of completion rather than inadequacy.
But here, perhaps, Christianity poses its greatest challenge to
us because it demands that we get off the fence and do something about it. We can no longer consider God a thing to argue
about rather than Someone to follow and obey.

Questions

1. What are some of the ways Carey suggests people are drawn to God? Can you suggest others?
2. What does Carey mean by a holistic approach to life?
3. Why is it inadequate to regard Christianity as an "add on" to life? How do people today treat Christianity that way?

3

Affirmations

How Do We Come to Know God?

Cornelius Plantinga, Jr.

Why do you believe in God? is a remarkably difficult question to answer. Still, says Cornelius Plantinga, Jr., Christians are convinced of God. The source of this unshakable conviction is a "hidden persuader."

Scripture

When we cry, "Abba! Father!" It is the Spirit himself bearing witness with our spirit that we are children of God.

—Romans 8:15,16

Confession

What, therefore, neither the light of nature nor the law could do, that God performs by the operation of the Holy Spirit through the word or ministry of reconciliation; which is the glad tidings concerning the Messiah. . . .

—Canons of Dort III-IV, Article 6

It is remarkably hard to answer the question,"Why do you believe in God?" So many answers do not seem quite final. You might say, for example, "I believe because my parents taught me." But that is not a final answer. Even wise parents are wrong about some things. They might have been wrong about God.

You might say, instead, "I believe in God because of the Bible and what it says about him." But, again, how do you know the Bible is right? Other books disagree with it.

Perhaps you could say, "I believe because God has actually sent his Son among us." But, once more, that answer seems unsatisfactory. After all, you learned about Christ from the

Bible—and the Bible has been set aside for the moment.

Well, then, suppose you say, "I believe because I can see evidence of design and providence in the world." That will not quite clinch the matter either. Perhaps the universe was designed by a beginning team of designers. They were pretty good. For example, they outfitted many creatures with an ingenious, built-in pump called a "heart." But they did not perfect it. So some creatures have heart failure.

When it comes right down to it, we are hard put to say how we know God. Yet we do. With all our heart we are convinced of God and his love and his determination to put things right in a world gone wrong.

How do we know? Perhaps the plainest thing to say, first, is that we have a strong inner conviction. We are *convinced* of God. And we discover that the Bible knows about this strange, unshakable conviction. It calls it the witness of the Holy Spirit.

As it turns out, the Spirit is the hidden persuader in all of our otherwise doubtful sources. It is the Spirit who stimulates childlike faith in what our parents say and do about God. The Spirit witnesses to the truth of the Scriptures, telling us in our hearts that "they are from God." The Spirit sparks faith in Jesus Christ, the Son of God. It is even the Holy Spirit who is brooding over our deep places when we ache with the sense of God in nature.

When in some moment of recognition we call God's name; when after years of prayerless life we begin again; "when we cry, 'Abba! Father!' it is the Spirit himself bearing witness with our spirit that we are children of God."

A Prayer or Hymn
> Creator Spirit, by whose aid
> The world's foundations first were laid,
> Come, visit every pious mind;
> Come, pour thy joys on human kind;
> From sin and sorrow set us free,
> And make thy temples worthy thee.
> —"Creator Spirit, by Whose Aid"

Questions

1. What are three common answers to the question "Why do you believe in God?"
2. Why are each of these three answers not quite final? How does the Holy Spirit use these "doubtful sources" to bring us to "unshakable conviction"?
3. How can a better understanding of the Holy Spirit strengthen a Christian's faith?
4. If you are a Christian, why do you believe in God?

Two Parables

Philip Yancey

Philip Yancey says that people have a choice to make. They live either as if God exists or as if he does not exist. In this selection he presents two stories that are parables of these alternatives. One is the story of a young boy who killed his father but later cried out for him. The other is Yancey's story of "discovering" his own father's love through a crumpled photograph.

[Here are] two stories, both of them true, which for me stand as parables for the alternatives: the way of faith and the way of non-faith.

The first comes from a sermon by Frederick Buechner:

It is a peculiarly twentieth-century story, and it is almost too awful to tell: about a boy of twelve or thirteen who, in a fit of crazy anger and depression, got hold of a gun somewhere and fired it at his father, who died not right away but soon afterward. When the authorities asked the boy why he had done it, he said that it was because he could not stand his father, because his father demanded too much of him, because he was always after him, because he hated his father. And then later on, after he had been placed in a house of detention somewhere, a guard was walking down the corridor late one night when he heard sounds from the boy's room, and he stopped to listen. The words that he heard the boy sobbing out in the dark were, "I want my father, I want my father."

Buechner says that this story is "a kind of parable of the lives of all of us." Modern society is like that boy in the house of detention. We have killed off our Father. Few thinkers or writers or moviemakers or television producers take God seriously anymore. He's an anachronism, something we've outgrown. The modern world has accepted The Wager and bet against God. There are too many unanswered questions. He has disappointed us once too often.

It is a hard thing to live, uncertain of anything. And yet, sobs can still be heard, muffled cries of loss, such as those expressed in literature and film and almost all modern art. The alternative to disappointment with God seems to be disappointment without God. ("The center of me," said Bertrand Russell, "is always and eternally a terrible pain—a curious wild pain—a searching for something beyond what the world contains.")

I see that sense of loss in the eyes of my friend Richard, even now. He says he does not believe in God, but he keeps bringing up the subject, protesting too loudly. From where comes this wounded sense of betrayal if no one is there to do the betraying?

Frederick Buechner's parable concerns the loss of a father; the second concerns the discovery of a father.

It too is a true story, my own story.

One holiday I was visiting my mother, who lives seven hundred miles away. We reminisced about times long past, as mothers and sons tend to do. Inevitably, the large box of old photos came down from the closet shelf, spilling out a jumbled pile of thin rectangles that mark my progression through childhood and adolescence: the cowboy-and-Indian getups, the Peter Cottontail suit in the first grade play, my childhood pets, endless piano recitals, the graduations from grade school and high school and finally college.

Among those photos I found one of an infant, with my name written on the back. The portrait itself was not unusual. I looked like any baby: fat-cheeked, half-bald, with a wild, unfocused look to my eyes. But the photo was crumpled and mangled, as if one of those childhood pets had got hold of it. I asked my mother why she had hung onto such an abused photo when she had so many other undamaged ones.

There is something you should know about my family: when I was ten months old, my father contracted spinal lumbar polio. He died three months later, just after my first birthday. My father was totally paralyzed at age twenty-four, his muscles so weakened that he had to live inside a large steel cylinder that did his breathing for him. He had few visitors—people had as much hysteria about polio in 1950 as they do about AIDS today. The one visitor who came faithfully, my mother, would sit in a certain place so that he could see her in a mirror bolted to the side of the iron lung.

My mother explained to me that she had kept the photo as a memento, because during my father's illness it had been fastened to his iron lung. He had asked for pictures of her and of his two sons, and my mother had had to jam the pictures in between some metal knobs. Thus, the crumpled condition of my baby photo.

I rarely saw my father after he entered the hospital, since children were not allowed in polio wards. Besides, I was so young that, even if I had been allowed in, I would not now retain those memories.

When my mother told me the story of the crumpled photo, I had a strange and powerful reaction. It seemed odd to imagine someone caring about me whom, in a sense, I had never met. During the last months of his life, my father had spent his waking hours staring at those three images of his family, my family. There was nothing else in his field of view. What did he do all day? Did he pray for us? Yes, surely. Did he love us? Yes. But how can a paralyzed person express his love, especially when his own children are banned from the room?

I have often thought of that crumpled photo, for it is one of the few links connecting me to the stranger who was my father, a stranger who died a decade younger than I am now. Someone I have no memory of, no sensory knowledge of, spent all day every day thinking of me, devoting himself to me, loving me as well as he could. Perhaps, in some mysterious way, he is doing so now in another dimension. Perhaps I will 1 have time, much time, to renew a relationship that was cruelly ended just as it had begun.

I mention this story because the emotions I felt when my mother showed me the crumpled photo were the very same emotions I felt that February night in a college dorm room when I first believed in a God of love. *Someone is there*, I realized. Someone is watching life as it unfolds on this planet. More, Someone is there who loves me. It was a startling feeling of wild hope, a feeling so new and overwhelming that it seemed fully worth risking my life on.

Questions

1. Why do you think the boy who hated and killed his father later cried for him?
2. Why did the crumpled photograph have such a powerful effect on Yancey? What did it mean to him? In what way was it symbolic?
3. Why did Yancey feel the same emotions when he first believed in God? How was his father's love like God's love?
4. How do the two parables relate to the theme of affirmation?

Seven Stanzas at Easter

John Updike

John Updike is a renowned American novelist, essayist, and poet. In this poem, from his collection Telephone Poles and Other Poems, *Updike challenges the reader to consider the physical evidences which seem to support the bodily resurrection of Christ.*

Make no mistake: if He rose at all
it was as His body;
if the cells' dissolution did not reverse, the molecules reknit,
    the amino acids rekindle,
 the Church will fall.

It was not as the flowers,
each soft Spring recurrent;
it was not as His Spirit in the mouths and fuddled eyes of the
    eleven apostles;
it was as His flesh: ours.

The same hinged thumbs and toes,
the same valved heart
that—pierced—died, withered, paused, and then regathered
    out of enduring Might
new strength to enclose.

Let us not mock God with metaphor,
 analogy, sidestepping, transcendence;
making of the event a parable, a sign painted in the faded
    credulity of earlier ages:
let us walk through the door.

The stone is rolled back, not papier-mâché,
not a stone in a story,
but the vast rock of materiality that in the slow grinding of
    time will eclipse for each of us
the wide light of day.

And if we will have an angel at the tomb,
make it a real angel,
weighty with Max Planck's quanta, vivid with hair, opaque in
    the dawn light, robed in real linen
spun on a definite loom.

Let us not seek to make it less monstrous,
for our own convenience, our own sense of beauty,
lest, awakened in one unthinkable hour, we are embarrassed
    by the miracle,
and crushed by remonstrance.

Questions

1. Do you think Updike is expressing faith or uncertainty in
    this poem? Why?
2. Why does he say "Let us not mock God with metaphor, /
    analogy, sidestepping, transcendence"? How would one
    do that?
3. What do you think is the "door" in the fourth stanza?
4. In the final stanza, what challenge does Updike leave with
    the reader?

Who Is in Control?

M. Howard Rienstra

M. Howard Rienstra was a history professor and scholar before his death from cancer in 1986. In this selection, he tells how he gave complete control of his life to Jesus Christ and how that decision resulted in deep personal assurance of his salvation. Three panic attacks during what should have been a fairly routine surgery brought Rienstra face to face with the reality of death. Afterward he confessed his resistance and "experienced God's pursuing grace."

The realization that one is dying comes slowly. Six years ago I was diagnosed as having cancer. I have non-Hodgkins lymphoma. I was assured that although it was third stage, it was nonetheless treatable. It has been, and on two occasions I was in remission. At one point I lost most of my hair, and I have done an awful lot of vomiting over these years. Yet I seemed to be in control. I knew that the vomiting was only temporary, and I could feel the lymph nodes return to normal as the chemotherapy took effect. I accepted the reality of my cancer, but I denied that I had really lost control over my own life. It seemed, in fact, as if I were not yet dying .

The beginnings of a change came near midnight this past January 30. My fever had risen to 104, and Mary was driving me to the hospital for the second time this year. I said to her, "You know, don't you, that one of these times when I go to the hospital I won't return?" She quietly said, "Yes." Without using the words "death" or "dying," we came to acknowledge the reality of it and that I was losing control—however reluctant my acknowledgment remained.

Early in April, after two hospitalizations had produced no clear reasons for continuing fever and lung problems, an outpatient lung biopsy was performed. A tube was placed in my lungs through which the doctor could both visually examine the lung and take small tissue samples for analysis. At the end I returned home, but my fever flared to 103 and so I was quickly back in the hospital. That first biopsy also failed to give any clear reason for my difficulties. It was decided, then, to do an open-chest biopsy. At this point the doctors were expecting to find cancer in the lung, but they were pleasantly surprised not to. The only certain thing was a mildly severe fibrosis of the lungs.

Failing to find anything specific to treat, the doctors' suspicion fell on the general condition of my cancer. I returned home, coughing and running intermittently high fevers. Mary and I recognized my worsening condition. We decided on the basis of the three hospitalizations that I would not return to the hospital again just to treat my fever and cough. I would rather die at home. We, in other words, were trying to regain control over my life, and even my death.

Later, however, because I had not received any chemotherapy since January 3, it was proposed that I begin a new kind of chemo, VP16, and on Thursday, May 2, an attempt was made. But my veins couldn't handle the chemical, and only half a dose was administered. I would have to have a Hickman catheter or a Port-a-Cath placed in my chest so that I could receive further chemo and quickly. Outpatient surgery was scheduled for the next Monday to install the Port-a-Cath.

Little did we know what would be the consequences of that decision. It seemed merely to be another decision made so I could stay in control. Dozens of such decisions had been made over the years. And this did not violate our no-hospitalization resolve, since I would walk in around noon and walk out by 4 p.m., having the procedure done with local anesthesia. Very simple. I was in control.

I was in the operating room promptly at 1 p.m., and after the usual preliminaries and administering of local anesthesia, the cutting in my neck began. The surgeon had externally seen and palpitated a vein which he thought would be appropriate.

Upon exposing that vein, however, he discovered it was too small to receive the catheter tubing. He then turned to other deeper veins. Let me anticipate questions by saying that I am an oddity. The veins in my neck, as it turns out, are not positioned as in an anatomy textbook. This structural oddity would soon have profound consequences.

The surgeon eventually found a large vein which he assumed to be the external jugular vein. For most people it would have been. But as he put the catheter in that vein it could not be positioned correctly. It ran off either to my left or right arm, but it wouldn't go straight down no matter what he tried. A properly structured external jugular vein would have gone down as far as it had to for the successful operation of the Port-a-Cath. This one wouldn't.

At this point, about two hours into the surgery, some dramatic things began to happen. I began to think that I was going to die. I heard my surgeon call for another surgeon to come to assist him. And the surgeons he named were the big names of Grand Rapids surgeons. At that point I began gasping for breath. In my perception I was panicking in the face of death. I said to Mary the next day, "I couldn't breathe, and they didn't know what to do about it." My whole body shook as I desperately fought for air. I asked for oxygen and was given it, but since I was breathing very shallowly, it took a while for even breathing to return and for my panic in the face of what I then thought was my imminent death to subside.

Before what finally was a four-and-a-half-hour operation was over, I went through two more similar episodes of panic and gasping for breath. I was scared to death and scared to die. I tried to pray, but couldn't. I tried to recite to myself my favorite childhood hymn, "What a Friend We Have in Jesus," but the words seemed empty. I was convinced I was dying, and I recognized more closely than ever before in my life that I was no longer in even apparent control. The loss of control came to me in the crudest of ways, as I voided my urine during each of the three episodes of panic and gasping for breath.

Meanwhile the second surgeon, an open-heart specialist,

came in and, having confirmed the oddity of my vein structure, scrubbed and took over the operation. He decided to go
after the internal jugular vein, which lies more deeply in the
neck. It was not easy, but after about an hour he had the
catheter successfully placed and the operation was then finished by the first surgeon.

I now know what had actually happened. I have been
assured that I didn't really panic, but that my body was in fact
seriously deprived of oxygen. Oxygen deprivation rather typi-
cally produces both the gasping for breath and the sense of
panic. That is the medical explanation. I was also informed
that if I had not been able to regain even breathing they would
simply have given me a general anesthesia in addition to the
local I was receiving. I accept these scientific explanations, and
it would be very tempting to substitute them for what I had
experienced. I could again think I was in control. But more
lessons were to come.

After four and a half hours of surgery I obviously was not
going to walk out of the hospital that day. In fact, they kept me
on 6 liters of oxygen; my fever continued to flare; and I was
coughing up heavy sputum. They ran a culture on that sputum, and remarkably for the first time since January a specific
infection was identified. It was pseudomonis, a rather bad
infection of the lungs.

It is now being treated successfully, but it would not have
been had I not stayed in the hospital. Rather, I would have
gone home, and the next afternoon, with the help of Tylenol, I
would have attended the semiannual meeting of the Govern-
ing Board of the Meeter Center for Calvin Studies. In fact, I
could not have seen a doctor until Thursday, when the second
stage of my new chemo was to be administered through my
new Port-a-Cath. Speculation is always dangerous about
things that did not happen, but it could be that if the chemo
had been administered, the pseudomonis would have
advanced to a fatal stage. By trying to stay in control I would
in fact have been committing suicide. Thus the experience of
dying which I had on the operating room table was really

God's way of extending my life and his clear demonstration to me that he and not I was in control.

Paradoxes are always difficult to understand. The paradox of good coming out of bad reminds me of John Milton's paradox of the "Fortunate Fall." Briefly, the fortunate fall argument is that if humankind had not fallen into sin, we would never have known the infinite love and mercy of God in Jesus Christ. In my case paradoxes abound. If when I was born I had a normal structure to my veins, I would now possibly be dying of pseudomonis without treatment. If my veins hadn't collapsed on Thursday I would not have had the Monday surgery with the same consequences. And even during the surgery, if I had not experienced the panic and gasping for breath, I would not have been willing to lose control. I had to be beaten out of my arrogant, selfish, and unbelieving sense of being in charge.

Thus the primary benefit—the real good that came out of the apparent evil—is neither physical nor psychological, but spiritual. My belief has been strengthened and my faith deepened as dying seemed so near and God so far away. Some background explanation is probably appropriate.

I have always believed, or so it seems. I have always had a sense of God's leading and directing my life. From the time of my adoption at age ten, there could be no doubt about that. Probability theory would be quite inadequate as an explanation of my life. I have had a strong faith and understanding of God's presence—but that faith and understanding were not, as I learned on the operating table, the full assurance of my salvation. To put it in terms that were popular a few years ago, I was still on the throne of my life rather than Christ. Intellectually I affirmed the Reformed faith without doubt and I took great delight in defending it. I have never intellectually doubted in the slightest the doctrines of the incarnation and resurrection of Christ, and I would with only slight provocation explain and defend them. And I have always known and taught the distinction between believing *that* Jesus Christ is God and believing *in* Jesus Christ. Salvation comes only from the latter.

What then went wrong? Knowing all that, teaching all that, and even trying in the practice of life to live justly, I still was trying to keep control. I refused to give myself over to Christ completely. I had to be broken for the comforting assurance of the first question and answer of the Heidelberg Catechism—that I am not my own but belong to my faithful Savior—to become a reality. It had always been real intellectually and even psychologically, but not spiritually, because I wanted to belong to myself—to stay in the driver's seat. Perhaps the best example of that is my never having prayed during these past six years for my own healing. I could pray for others, but not for myself. To pray for healing for myself would be to lose control—and God who knows the secrets of our hearts would surely not receive the prayers of one who was yet resisting him.

My brokenness began on the operating table on Monday and continued on Tuesday as I confessed my resistance in tearful prayer with Mary, and then continued the same with my minister. The assurance of salvation began to become a reality as I experienced God's pursuing grace so vividly. I am not, except in the most common biblical sense, a saint. Nor do I anticipate changes in belief or in the practice of life that will be visible to others. But I have been spiritually transformed by the grace of God coming through these paradoxical experiences. I now know more than intellectually that I am not in control, that I do not belong to myself. I have the comfort of the Heidelberg Catechism and of God's real presence.

And all this because of an odd neck.

Questions

1. Why had Rienstra lived as if he were in control of his life? What circumstances led to his giving control over to Jesus?
2. Will Jesus settle for only partial control of a believer's life? Why is his way "all or nothing"?
3. Rienstra was a very intelligent person. He was a student of the Bible and delighted in explaining and defending Chris-

tian beliefs. Does it surprise you that he still did not have full assurance of his salvation as he went into the surgery? What can you learn from Rienstra's experience?

4. If you are a Christian, where does your assurance of salvation lie?

Acknowledgments

Worldviews

"Worldviews: An Overview" from *Discipleship of the Mind* by James W. Sire. Copyright © 1990 by James W. Sire. Reprinted by permission of InterVarsity Press, P.O. Box 1400, Downers Grove, IL 60515.

"A Victim of Spiritual Poverty" from *Harvard Diary: Reflections on the Sacred and Secular* by Robert Coles. Copyright © 1988 by Robert Coles and the New Oxford Review. Reprinted by permission of the Crossroad Publishing Company.

"Origins" from *The Naked Ape: A Zoologist's Study of the Human Animal* by Desmond Morris. Reprinted by permission of McGraw-Hill, Inc.

"The Drugstore Curse" from *The Woman Warrior* by Maxine Hong Kingston. Copyright © 1975, 1976 by Maxine Hong Kingston. Reprinted by permission of Alfred A. Knopf, Inc.

"Psalm 8" from NIV Study Bible. Reprinted by permission of Zondervan Publishing House.

"Preamble—Our World Belongs to God." Reprinted by permission of CRC Publications.

Common Objections to the Christian Faith

Introductory Readings

"Still Looking: Will Rob Find Faith?" by Chris Lutes from *Campus Life* Magazine, Christianity Today, Inc. Copyright © 1989. Reprinted by permission.

"Why We Believe" from *How to Give Away Your Faith* by Paul Little. Copyright © 1988 by Marie Little. Reprinted by permission of InterVarsity Press, P.O. Box 1400, Downers Grove, IL 60515.

"Giving Reasons for Our Faith" from *Out of the Saltshaker and Into the World* by Rebecca Manley Pippert. Copyright © 1979 by InterVarsity Christian Fellowship of the U.S.A. Reprinted by permission of InterVarsity Press., P.O. Box 1400, Downers Grove, IL 60515.

How Can I Believe in Such an Exclusive Religion?

"Why I'm Not a Christian: A Report" by Robert Kachur. Reprinted from *HIS* magazine, February 1986, © 1986 by IVCF. Used by permission.

"No Escape" from *Reason to Believe* by R.C. Sproul. Copyright © 1978 by G/L Publications, copyright transferred in 1981 to R.C. Sproul. Reprinted by permission of Zondervan Publishing House.

"Is Jesus the Only Way?" by Darrell Johnson from *The Campus Evangelism Handbook* edited by Andres Tapia. Copyright © 1987 by *U* Magazine. Reprinted by permission of InterVarsity Press, P.O. Box 1400, Downers Grove, IL 60515.